My
Beautiful Garden

My Beautiful Garden

Exposing

The Secrets For

Successful Marriage and Family Life

KENN MARK

authorHOUSE®

AuthorHouse™
1663 Liberty Drive
Bloomington, IN 47403
www.authorhouse.com
Phone: 1-800-839-8640

© *2011 by Kenn Mark. All rights reserved.*

No part of this book may be reproduced, stored in a retrieval system, or transmitted by any means without the written permission of the author.

First published by AuthorHouse   07/19/2011

ISBN: 978-1-4567-8538-3 (sc)
ISBN: 978-1-4567-8553-6 (ebk)

Printed in the United States of America

Any people depicted in stock imagery provided by Thinkstock are models, and such images are being used for illustrative purposes only.
Certain stock imagery © *Thinkstock.*

This book is printed on acid-free paper.

Because of the dynamic nature of the Internet, any web addresses or links contained in this book may have changed since publication and may no longer be valid. The views expressed in this work are solely those of the author and do not necessarily reflect the views of the publisher, and the publisher hereby disclaims any responsibility for them.

CONTENTS

Foreword vii
Dedication ix
Acknowledgments xi
Introduction xiii
Preface xvii

Part One—Building Your Home On The Right Foundation

Chapter 1: What's Special About Home 3
Chapter 2: Building A Kingdom Driven Home 10
Chapter 3: What's Special about Marriage? 17

Part Two—Pillars Of Marriage

Chapter 4: Things That Makes For Successful Marriage 27
Chapter 5: When The Heart Beat Is One 38
Chapter 6: Your Wife Needs A Husband 42
Chapter 7: Your Husband Needs A Wife 46

Part Three—Building Your Home According To Pattern

Chapter 8: Planning For Your Home 53
Chapter 9: Ingredients Of Good Parenting 61

Part Four—Building Your Home With The Right Building Blocks

Chapter 10: Punishment Or Discipline?... 67

Part Five—Ceiling Your Marriage With Love

Chapter 11: Sex And Romance In Marriage 77

Bibliography.. 85
About The Book.. 87
About The Author... 89
Re: My Beautiful Garden 91

FOREWORD

Marriage is a gift from God and has been identified as the most important of human relationships. God instituted it for the joy and happiness of mankind. The marriage institution and family life have come under serious attack in recent times. Many marriages are crumbling about to break. Many have collapsed and left the family members hurting. No amount of information on how to help participants and players in this institution get the most out of it, will be too much. This explains why this book titled ***"My Beautiful Garden"*** by Rev. Kenn Mark is just appropriate and expedient.

I recommend this to every married couple and those contemplating to build a viable home through Christian type of marriage or any other type of marriage by this I mean those who would dare to practice the principles of the Holy Bible with respect to marriage and family life. It is highly recommended for every library and all who cherish the marriage institution.

Ven. Obioma Onwuzurumba
Chaplain, Aso Villa Chapel. Abuja, Nigeria.

DEDICATION

I whole heartily dedicate this work to God Almighty who is the builder and keeper of every beautiful home.

To the memory of my late beloved Daddy, Prof. Mark Igboeli who gave me a picture of what a lovely home should look like.

ACKNOWLEDGMENTS

I gladly wish to express my heartfelt appreciation and thanks to these dear ones:

My lovely wife Madeline, who believed so much in my vision and has been very supportive in my book writing, offering helpful ideas in the entire process. You are a blessing to me; may you be eternally fulfilled in all things. My lovely sons, Praise and Dominion have been so encouraging and understanding as well. They often hang around me while the work was on; making positive input. I pray that the good Lord will cause you to find favour with God and with men. My caring Mum, Selina and my siblings have made an unforgettable impart to my ministry and call, may heaven remember you for eternal blessing. My fathers in Christ: Ven. Obioma Onwuzurumba, Bishop Godson, Pst. Sam Odaudu have helped to shape, guide and helped me to go this far, may the Almighty God promote you beyond your widest imagination. To my General Overseer, Pst. Enoch Adeboye, you are my role model, may you find eternal fulfilment in God.

To all my friends in ministry and my children in the Lord, especially the family of RCCG Dominion Gate Parish, you are my joy, my comfort and my boast in the Lord. May the unsearchable riches of God in Christ Jesus be sufficient for you in all good things. Shalom.

INTRODUCTION

Building an unshakable home is a highest level of sacrifice; the responsibility to turn your marriage "for better" or "for worse" is yours. If you don't do something, nothing gets done.

What shall it profit a man or a woman to gain the whole world but lose his or her home?. ?. There have been various inspirational books that have been written by several great authors ranging from Bible scholars to sociologists from ancient era to the present post modern time on the topic—marriage and family life.

"He who made them in the beginning made them male and female . . . what God has joined together, let no man put asunder" Mt.19:4-6.

In one of his famous quotes, Buddha has it that a family is a place where people come into contact with each other and if they love each other the home will be a beautiful garden. But in case these people lose harmony, it resembles a storm that creates havoc in the garden. This is a proof that the belief that the home should be a place where harmony should prevail cuts across all faiths, while the channel of achieving such harmony may differ.

The most important decision that mankind (though not all) must make in life after the decision for deeper relationship with God is the choice for the right marriage partner and on how to raise a joyful family. This is because your choice of life partner will go a long way in determining and shaping your destiny on earth. Therefore, the challenge of this post modern world is how to cope with the fast declining moral values in the society and the concomitant influence it exerts on marriage and family life. We are in an era characterized by a shift in family values and biblical order.

> *"For I know the thoughts {divine agenda} that I think toward you, saith the Lord, thoughts of peace, (solace) and not of evil, to give you an expected end."*
>
> **Jer. 29:11**

The ultimate plan of God in His divine agenda is to make our homes a place where people can find solace; so that His will be done just as it is done in heaven. The home is a very powerful agent of change. The transformation that our society desires and deserves is rooted in the very foundation of the home. God has strategically positioned the home as a shaper and moulder of destinies. The greatest responsibility of a post modern home is to confront the rapidly declining moral values and spiritual bankruptcy in our present day society.

This explains the reason for the upsurge in marriage break down, family disintegration, spouse abuse, child abuse, drug abuse, domestic violence, drunkenness, and all the concomitant vices that has pervaded our world today. The sad news is that if the home is weakened, a generation is lost and the society becomes hopeless. **It is popular to hear in many Christian marriages, "till death do us part"; in reality, many couples today seem to be saying "till divorce do us part".** Research and statistics has shown that for every five marriages conducted today, about two often end up in divorce. It has also been discovered that spouses especially women who die as a result of injuries inflicted on them by their spouses outnumbers those who die through any other form of accident.

One incident from the innumerable others is the report on BBC news 17.00 o'clock, of 5th, March, 2010, about a man that stabbed his wife to death after few months of being released from cell for attempted murder of his former partner. It is more pathetic to note that Christian families are not spared from this beast of domestic violence. Children today are raised up in a very toxic environment. Many of them watch dad and mum fight; while some see Daddy or Mummy killed or brutalized by those they exchanged marital vows with. Children raised in such homes are often exposed to all forms of child abuse and eventually grow up to be terrors to the society.

This shift in biblical culture and marital pattern has permeated every segment of the society. The doctrine of Gay marriage, lesbianism and pluralism is not only welcome by the society, but it is now accepted by the tenet of faith of some "churches". These are nothing but signs of an amoral society.

It is sad to note that the innocence of our children is unknowingly exploited by the emergence of the post modern culture. Children are now given the liberty to make choices on the path they want to lead in life with minimal or no supervision and guidance by parents. This emerging trend is a satanic onslaught to divine order and absolutely in contradiction to the word of God. Read:

> *"Train up a child in the way he should go; and when he is old, he will not depart from it."*
> **Prov.22:7**

The mandate of training, nurturing, shaping, guiding, mentoring and disciplining a child is a responsibility handed over to parents by our creator and maker, the almighty God. Sadly, our society has become too permissive and Christian principles have been pushed to a corner. Some societies have gone a step forward to withdraw the right of parents to discipline their children. Such bill is sponsored and promoted from the pit of hell to rob our children of their morals.

The level of decadence in the family today is so pathetic that even politicians can not bottle up their worries. The present Prime minister of United Kingdom, David Cameron as quoted by Babatunde Adedibu in his book *Storytelling an Effective Communication Appeal in Preaching* observed on 7th July 2008 at Glasgow "that is why our children are growing up without boundaries, thinking they can do as they please, and why no adult will intervene to stop them—including, often, their parents"

Lamenting on the declining state of male role models in the family, the first black president of the United State, Barracks Obama, in his speech on the annual father's day in America on 15th June, 2008 as observed also by Babatunde Adedibu, *Storytelling An Effective Communication Appeal In Preaching,* has this to say, "too many fathers are also missing—missing from too many lives and too many homes. They have abandoned their responsibilities, acting like boys instead of men and the foundation of their family has suffered because of it"

Do we fold our hands or throw in the towel and allow this beast of postmodernism to vomit its venom on our marriages and family lives? No! We must rise to the challenge. This is the vision behind this project. The writer is on a divine mission to restore the sacredness of the marriage institution and to give the home a strong foundation or rock on which to stand. This assignment is called "operation rescue the home". The chapters are segmented to answer the questions of both the married and unmarried readers. Children, preachers, marriage counsellors and every one who truly desires guidance for marriage and family life will find this book very helpful. As you go through this book, I pray that your home will receive a divine and positive turn around.

PREFACE

Building your marital home is synonymous to building your physical home. It will require the same skill, wisdom, patience and labour in laying a strong foundation, carving the pillars, putting the right building blocks and ceiling the roof.

On coming to the United Kingdom, my first shock was seeing the fast rate at which families are disintegrating and breaking up. Broken hearts and shattered lives pervade the entire society. Many children live without love and direction and the society is paying dearly for this anomaly: The media is flooded with news of rape, murder, stabbing, drug abuse and unbridled passion for crime and delinquency as a result of bringing up children in a toxic environment.

If there is any institution that has been badly battered by the post modern order, it is marriage and family life. Today, many young men and women dread marriage, choosing rather to remain single or to become civil partners. This is nothing but escapism. Trying to avoid the reality of the problem is a bigger problem in its self. Someone has got to say no to the corrupt order; the time to retrace our path back to God's way is now. Our post-modern system and cultural shift has failed us, common sense and human solution has disappointed us. It's time to go back to God's original purpose for the home.

We have to take a look at God's original plan for marriage and family life; this is because the family is the root of a nation. We have to come into terms with things that bring stability and joy to the home. Many have asked these questions—How can we beat divorce? What must we do to restore peace and fulfilment in our marriages? Why are some children rebellious while others, conformists? The answers to these questions could be traced to the foundation of our marriages.

> *"If the foundation be destroyed, what can the righteous do?"*
> **Ps.11:3**

The change and spiritual bankruptcy the world is witnessing today which is also shaking the foundation of homes is not strange to any student of the Bible. The Bible is vocal about the changes that will occur in this end time known by researchers as the post modern era or the second modern world.

> *"This know also, that in the last days, perilous times shall come. For men shall be lovers of their own selves (gays), covetous, boastful, proud, blasphemers (of God and the Bible), disobedient to parents, unthankful, unholy, without natural affection, trucebreakers, false accusers, incontinent, fierce, despisers of those that are good (and godly lifestyle) traitors, heady, high-minded (insisting on their own ways), lovers of pleasures more than lovers of God; having a form of godliness, but denying the power thereof: from such turn away"*
> **2Tim.3:1-5**

The only option in dealing with this tragedy is for the Christian home to devise a new strategy of combating the spirit of this age. This is the aim of this book. This problem is not race or tribal bound; it is ubiquitous, it affects every nation, tribe and religion and behoves urgent remedy. If we can by His grace and mercy build a God centred home, then we can boast of a God centred society; if we can have a God centred society, then we can enjoy a God centred world. **The baton starts from your home.**

> *"Except the Lord builds a house, they labour in vain that build it: except the Lord keeps the city, the watchman waketh but in vain."*
> **Ps.127:1**

PART ONE

BUILDING YOUR HOME ON THE RIGHT FOUNDATION

Building your Marriage is like building a house. If the foundation is weak, the entire building faces the threat of collapse. On what foundation is your home built?

CHAPTER 1

What's Special about Home

A Home VS A House.

When I was younger, I had a friend whose experience taught me a lesson which formed the burden that generated my vision for librating homes and families. It's over twenty years now that I saw Michael or heard anything about him, yet he made a comment which has refused to part with me all these years. I went to visit Michael one of those days in his family house. As I approach the gate, I was almost intimidated by the architectural design of what looked like a castle "could this be Michael's house?" I kept asking myself as I walked closer to check the house number enshrined on the massive gate. At this point, I could observe the beautiful flowers with different colours, a well designed orchard and garden with varieties of fruits. This almost made me wonder how heaven will look like. I'd known Michael then for about a year but he had never for one day said anything about his home.

On realizing that the number at the gate was the same with the number I had in my address book, I proceeded to press the bell, this time I was smiling and ready to embrace my friend. After waiting outside the gate for close to fifteen minutes, the cold wind of the season in northern Nigeria was now having its toil on me. I contemplated pressing the bell for the last time when I saw Michael peeping through the window upstairs like a thief locked in a cell. He was shocked to know that I was the one at the gate, without any pretence, he beckoned on me to run for my life before his father will catch up with me. I left without looking back.

The next day, Michael visited me to apologize and then for the first time, he told me the story about his family. "What you saw yesterday was just a house and not a home" he said "how do you mean?" I queried, "You told me to run before your dad meets . . ." before I could finish speaking, he interrupted, now almost moved to tears, he told me things I can not put down for obvious reasons, but the summary, is that after the death of his mother, the father married another woman who treated him and his younger ones like criminals in their father's house and succeeded in turning their father's heart against them.

Michael's misery was so terrible that the last time I asked about him some years ago, I was reliably told that he ran away from his fathers house and no one could trace his where about. Michael's words never made much sense to me then, but now I have come to accept the reality that there is a difference between a home and a house.

A home is generally known as a place where people live, but it is not enough to define a home as a place where a person lives, the Oxford English Dictionary was careful to add ". . . a place where a person was born or where they feel they belong, a place where those who need help are looked after." **A house becomes a home when it is inhabited by people who truly care for one another, people who are related by blood, marriage or adoption; people who may perform different roles but the same purpose and goal and share a sense of belonging.** I believe that every home that will achieve these tasks and withstand the storms or pressures of this age must be founded on the principles of love, joy, unity, peace and purpose. These are the features that distinguish a home from a house.

A domain of Love

Love is not just about giving, but giving up

An old adage has it that, "charity begins at home". No one can be more loving than they are in their home, if you do, that is hypocrisy. Love is not just about giving but giving up what you cherish most. The home is designed to be a domain of love. Love is one word that often seems difficult to define. Some have tried defining it only from the emotional perspective of feeling. Feeling is not the true test of love, though it could be part of it. It is not in the interest of this book to do a thorough exposition on love, yet is important to state for clarity sake that there are four Greek words that the Scripture used to explain love: **eros, phileo, starge and agape**. If you must enjoy your marriage and family life, you need the mixture of these various kinds of love.

Eros is a physical, passionate and sexual kind of love. It is healthy for couples and not for unmarried folks. **Phileo** is the love that thrives on closeness, companionship, sharing and partnership. It adds colour to marriage and family life and binds the husband and wife together in friendship union (Couples should relate as friends). This type of love is also known as brotherly or sisterly love. **Starge** is a family kind of love; it creates a feeling of loyalty, unity and oneness. It binds parents and children together to form a happy home. **Agape** is the kind of love that demands above every other thing that couples should give selflessly to each other in every ramification of life. It says love your spouse even when he or she seems unlovable:

> *Love (agape) is patient and kind. Love (agape) is not jealous or boastful or proud or rude. Love (agape) does not demand its own way. Love (agape) is not irritable, and it keeps no record of when it has been wronged . . . love (agape) never gives up, never loses faith, is always hopeful and endures through every circumstance.*
>
> **(Tropical Study Bible)**
>
> 1Cor.13:4-7

This is the love that binds the church to Christ. It requires sacrifice and commitment:

> *"Husbands, love (agape) your wives, even as Christ also loved (agape) the church, and gave himself for it"*
> Eph. 5:25,
>
> *"that they may teach the young women to be sober, to love(agape) their husbands, to love(sturge) their children, to*

> *be discreet, chaste, keepers at home, good, obedient to their own husbands, that the word of God be not blasphemed."*
> Tit.2:4-5

The desire to love is divine but is often abused by human manipulation. Love is the basis of any true relationship most especially family relationship. True love seeks the welfare and well being of others. It does not ask what shall I benefit from this relationship, rather what shall I bring into this relationship. It is unfortunate that many go into marriage today with selfish ambition. If the purpose for your marriage is all about what you can get from your spouse; you are laying a strong foundation for a broken home.

Love is having to say "I am sorry" over and over. It doesn't say "I apologised the other time; it is now your turn". Show me a home without love, and I will show you a people living in a house—not a home. Love appreciates. **The true test of love is not how much you are able to give but how much you are able to give up for the sake of the one you love.** Your relationship might not work until you are willing to give up your pride, arrogance and self centeredness. Read this:

> **"Don't ask your spouse constantly if he or she loves you. Although hearing the words is important, nagging your spouse for that affirmation will backfire. Ask yourself how you show your love. If your spouse is constantly asking you to profess your love, perhaps you are not saying it enough!"**
> ***Sheri and Bob Stritof***

The Beacon of Joy

Joy is what everyone desires in a home. A home where there is no joy is like living in hell. Many homes have pushed youths into all manners of crimes and anti social behaviours because joy has travelled from the house. The outcome is youths roaming about the street, looking for fun and joy from wrong places. When parents spend the whole time quarrelling and fighting each other, the children often become victims of hate and hurt.

I read with great pain and shock the story of the two brothers of 11 and 10, who tortured, battered and almost killed two other terrified young boys as reported in the Daily Mirror newspaper of 22nd of January, 2010. During interview with the police, the boys disclosed that they were bored, in other words, they wanted fun. It was later discovered that the boys in question grew up in a "nightmare environment, their drug addicted mum was regularly beaten by their drunken father in front of them" the children were also reported to be victims of their father's fury, "often forcing them to run from the house". A social worker summed it up, "the boys are victims of a toxic home life".

The home has a very important role to play in shaping the attitude of the man, the woman or the child on the street, at work or school. This is why God designed the home to be a beacon of joy. In such homes, husbands will not negotiate for extra time at work, because he is in a hurry to go home and spend more time with his joyful family. Wives will eagerly look forward to seeing her family spending good time together. The unfailing key to joy in the home will be discussed in chapter four.

The bond of Unity

Never compete with your spouse; compliment each other on your roles in the home.

The home is intended by God to be the bond of unity. If children can identify daddy's property and the ones bought by mummy, it is enough proof that the home is far from being united. Whenever we purchase any property in our home, my wife and I don't go arguing about who has ownership of what in the house, everything including our money is for us, not for me or for her. It amazes me when I hear some men talking to their wives or wives responding to their husbands and what you hear are "my car", "my house", "my fridge", "my money" and the rest of such words that a school boy rightly called "aggressive pronouns". Where is the place for oneness?

This was a lesson I learnt from my wife. When I relocated to London, I was out of job for sometime and was almost bankrupt. My wife virtually carried the financial load of the family, yet she never disrespected me. I was to go for a training which would cost quite some amount of money. I was reluctant to approach my wife on this, but eventually, I had to ask "Honey do you still have some money in your account?" "Do you mean our account?" she asked, "yes", I said laughing "our account". My wife had to bring my memory back to our marriage agreement that there is no me, but us. I pray God gives you oneness mentality in your marriage.

Unity and oneness in marriage is not only about bearing the same surname, but thinking together, planning together, playing together, crying together and in fact, doing every thing together.

Unity in Diversity

"Morning person or night owl; disorganized or neat nik; likes pets or hates pets—there is no right or wrong, good or bad. These are not faults, but differences. Learn to cope with and enjoy how different you each are."
Sheri and Bob Stritof

Celebrate your diversity, differences, strengths, gifting, and talents. You have something that is lacking in your wife; your wife as well has some qualities that are scarce in you, so also are the children. **Everyone matters in the home, no matter how much a man tries, he can never be a father and a mother to his children and the same applies to the wife.**

When my first son was less than two years, my wife had to unavoidably travel to the United Kingdom while I stayed behind with our first son. While she was in the United Kingdom, our second son was born. I was forced to play the role of the father and mother to our son—Praise in Nigeria, while my wife played the role of a mother and a father to Dominion in London. No matter how we tried, it was becoming so obvious from the behaviours of our kids that all was not well. Thank God that the enemy never put us to shame. **You can not be a father and a mother at the same time; we must complement and encourage each other.**

Read this:

> **"A healthy relationship is one in which two people encourage each other to reach their respective goals while sharing each others' hopes and dreams. A relationship should be a source of inspiration, invigoration and hope."**
>
> *Daisaku Ikeda.,*

God's divine arrangement is for couples to utilise each other's gifts, talents and experience in building their family life. Never look down on your spouse, no matter how sophisticated you may appear, rather give room for honour and learn from each other. Children are also wonderful assets to learn from. More will be discussed on this in chapter five—When the Heart Is One.

CHAPTER 2

Building a Kingdom Driven Home

What drives your home?

"The greatest tragedy is not death, but life without purpose"
Rick Warren

Being homeless is not the greatest tragedy but being in a home without a purpose. A popular adage has it that "a man's home is his castle", and "how a man lays his bed, so shall he lie on it". In building your home, it is important to know that it is not about getting married and producing offspring; it is about building a kingdom. In the beginning, the original plan and purpose of God for every home is to be an extension of His kingdom where God is the king and the ruler.

> "And God said; let us make man in our image, after our likeness: **and let them have dominion over the fish of the sea, and over the fowl of the air and over the cattle, and over all the earth, and over every creeping thing that creepeth upon the earth.** So God created man in his own image, in the image of God created he him; male and female created he them. And God blessed them, and God said unto them, be fruitful, and multiply, and replenish the earth, and subdue it: and have dominion over the fish of the sea, and over the fowl of the air, and over every living thing that moveth upon the earth."
> Gen. 1:26-28

The first command and blessing of God on man was for man to have dominion, *"and God blessed them and said unto them 'be fruitful and multiply, and replenish the earth, and subdue it: and have dominion . . ."* **fruitfulness is the first step to dominion**. Fruitfulness here transcends biological fruitfulness. It also includes financial fruitfulness, physical fruitfulness, emotional and otherwise. The original Hebrew word for fruitfulness is "productivity". On the other hand, dominion in the Hebrew translation is "rudah", which is synonymous to power, authority, victory, etc. It means to prevail, conquer and to rule. The purpose of God for initiating vision for the home is to give man (Adam and Eve) the authority to rule the earth and establish the righteousness of God.

The desire of God for the home is to establish dominion through marriage. God is still interested in raising a people that will build and establish his kingdom on earth so that families can witness the true righteousness, peace and joy in the Holy Ghost.

> *"And hast made us unto our God kings and priests: and we shall reign on the earth"*
> Rev.5:10

How to Build a Kingdom Driven Home

A kingdom driven home is a home driven by God's word, prayers, righteousness, peace and joy. In such homes, wives are to be treated as queens; husbands are to be treated as kings and children nurtured as princes and princesses.

Things that are not for kings

> *"Give not thy strength unto women, nor thy ways to that which destroyeth kings. It is not for kings, O Lamuel, it is not for kings to drink wine; nor for princes, strong drink: lest they drink, and forget the law, and pervert the judgement of any of the afflicted."*
> Prov.31:3-5

Adultery is not for kings and queens. When a man or woman indulges in adultery, that fellow is giving his or her strength to others. If you know your identity as a royal priesthood, you will place high level of respect and dignity upon your self and your marriage. On the other hand, our society today is filled with high level of drunkenness. This is because many have lost touch with their true identity as kings, queens, princes and princesses. When we become driven by the principles of God's kingdom, then we can experience a taste of heaven in our homes.

Driven By the Word

A kingdom driven home is a home founded on the principles of the word of God. The height of fulfilment, you will attain in your family will greatly be determined by the foundation on which your home is laid. People have different things on which they lay the foundation of their home. For some it is culture or tradition, for others family belief or experience, yet others lay the foundation of their home on the advice of friends or on what they see in movies. How solid are these foundations. Beloved, I encourage you to study the God's word. It is the unfailing blue print or the maker's manual for your marriage.

The word of God is the solid Rock which can carry, support and sustain your home.

> *"Except the Lord builds a house, they labour in vain that build it: except the Lord keeps the city, the watchman waketh but in vain."*
> Ps.127:1

Any home that is not standing on the word of God is not founded on the rock and could collapse at any moment. This is the misery behind the numerous broken homes in our society today. Not even you or your spouse or any other person has the final say on how your family should be run but the word of God. **Stop running your home with human ideologies; build your home on the principle of God's word.**

Driven By Prayers

Another secret of stability in the home is prayers. A family soaked in prayers will stand to defeat the beast of domestic violence and spirit of waywardness. **The greatest investment you can make for your children is to invest in prayers.**

I know a respected Christian couple, so dedicated to the service of the Lord, pastors and founders of a church with several thousand memberships but their son was a deviant and a drug addict. This couple tried every possible means to neutralize this negative influence and challenging behaviour which their son obviously picked from his peers, yet it appears as if the more they tried, the more the boy became worst.

One day, the young man approached his daddy and demanded he hand over his {the daddy} car key to him. At this time, his eyes were blood red, a proof that he was under the influence of drugs. When the daddy hesitated, the son brought out a well sharpened knife and threatened to stab the father. At this juncture, he forcefully snatched the key from the panicking father and off he went with friends to night club. After drinking and getting drunk they jumped into the father's car and zoomed off.

That was the last time the father saw or heard about the son for years. But daddy and mummy never stopped praying for their son. Night vigils were organised in the church for God to rescue the soul of this young man. It was like nothing was happening, no news of the son, yet they were not discouraged, they prayed the more. One day, like the story of the biblical prodigal son, this young man staggered home, but this time around, he was a completely different person. God literally snatched him from hell as a result of the prayers of the saint. Today, he is a pastor.

Driven By Righteousness

"And the Lord said, shall I hide from Abraham that thing which I do; seeing that Abraham shall surely become a great and mighty nation, and all the nations of the earth shall be blessed in him? For I know him that he will command his children and his household after him, and they shall keep the way of the Lord, to do justice and judgement, that the Lord may bring upon Abraham that which he has spoken of him."
Gen. 18:17-19

The post modern age in which we are is an era of moral decay, a death of righteousness and rationality, an amoral society where choice is celebrated above truth. We are living in a time where godliness is replaced by worldliness and many homes and families care more about mundane things more than they care about spiritual things. This is the age the Bible called "the perilous time"-2tim3:1-7

The purpose of God for the Christian home is to be a model of righteousness. Any home founded on righteousness is a home founded on Christ Jesus. The Righteousness of Christ is different from morality. Morality is self effort to do things right. In as much as it is good to be morally good, it is still best to establish your home on the foundation of Christ righteousness which is an imputed righteousness.

The Christian home is intended by God to be a place of bringing up godly children Abraham became the friend of God simply because God knew *"that he will command his children and his household after him, and they shall keep the way of the Lord, to do justice and judgement"*. It is recorded that God said; *"For I know him."* Can God boast of you that he knows you? You can be a friend of God by living a righteous life and shaping your home on the foundation of righteousness. Read this:

> *"Thy throne oh Lord is forever and ever, the sceptre of thy kingdom is a right sceptre, thy loveth righteousness and hated wickedness . . ."*
> Ps.45:6-7

Driven By Peace

"Seek peace and pursue it"
Ps.34:14

The family is divinely positioned to be a solace arena with the man and wife forming a solace union. This is the divine agenda in Jer. 29:11 *"For I know the thoughts {divine agenda} that I think toward you, saith the Lord, thoughts of peace, (solace) and not of evil, to give you an expected end."*

My Beautiful Garden

"The ideal family is a haven from the dangers of the larger world," says John J Macionis, a professor of Sociology. It is sad to note that domestic violence has taken over the place of peace in many homes today. In the words of sociologist Richard J Gelles,

> **"The family is the most violent group in society with the exception of the police and the military. You are more likely to get killed, injured, or physically attacked in your home by someone you are related to than in any other social context. In fact if violence were a communicable disease, the government would consider it an epidemic".**
> Cited in Roesch 1984:75

Writing further, Macionis observed that Government statistics show that almost 30percent of female murder victims and 6 percent of male murder victims are done by spouse. He noted that women stand the risk of being injured by a family member than they are to be mugged or raped by a stranger or injured in an automobile accident.

The church must passionately stand up to teach and to defend the divine purpose of God setting up the home which is to be a haven of peace. Some years ago, there was a conference organised in Nigeria on how to achieve inter religious peace in one of the northern states of the country. Speaking during the conference, a Christian elder states man stated **"peace is not a concept but a person, if you must have peace in you or in the state, you must give room in your heart for the Prince of peace"**.

I want to state clearly here that the pre-requisite to family peace is when couples or family members allow the true peace of Christ to over shadow them, at that point, members are willing to give up personal rights and pride for the over all peace of the home. It is a pity that our government and society in general often miss it by "seeking for the living in the midst of the dead", they set up different organizations for cubing domestic violence yet Jesus, the Prince of peace is sent packing from our homes, schools and society.

A practical and realistic plan for peace is the beginning of joy and happiness in homes.

Kenn Mark

Peace does not come by imagination, but by seeking it and pursuing it. There must be a desire for it, but desire alone does not create peace. Planning for peace requires you to understand and pursue after the things that makes for peace.

CHAPTER 3

What's Special about Marriage?

The Essence of Marriage

Don't go into wedlock until you understand the divine essence of marriage; once it's locked, you might not find a window of escape.

The most abused institution today is the marriage institution. Many people go into marriage for selfish reasons—some see marriage as a tool for solving immigration problems, some are looking for business partners and not life partners, others want to marry because that sister or brother will be suitable for "their ministry", some marry because they want to make children, some see marriage as a tool of escaping societal disrespect. I have interacted with some fellows who see money or wealth as a criterion for choosing life partner. They have forgotten that money has wings.

It is also necessary to note that there are those looking for sex partners and not destiny or marriage partners, little wonder in some developed countries, the word "partner" has taking over the use of the concept "husband and wife". People now get married to same sex and some so called churches are willing to wed them. Our churches and the society at large are now reluctant to offer a vocal condemnation on this evil in the name of "equal opportunity" and respect for "human right". The basic question is—why do you want to get married? Is it for selfish purpose or for God's purpose? If you are marrying in accordance with God's will, then do it the Lord's way.

> *"Good marriages create happy individuals and families, stronger communities, and a more stable society."*
> **Sheri and Bob Stritof**

Why On Earth Do I Want To Marry?

> *"Success in marriage does not come merely through finding the right mate, but through being the right mate."*
> Barnett R. Brickner

We can not understand fully the essence of marriage until we understand the meaning of marriage. So many people have tried defining marriage to fit into their personal desire and ambition. Nevertheless, God's order stands firm. Marriage is the union of a man and woman in holy matrimony, as a means of fulfilling their divine purpose on earth, through the consent of the couple and their parents. From the above definition, it is evident that God intended marriage to be a monogamous union

> *"He who made them in the beginning made them male and female . . . what God has joined together, let no man put asunder"*
> Mt.19:4-6

The originator of marriage says "let no man put asunder", but is it not obvious that today, people are putting asunder the original plan of God for marriage? God originally designed marriage for a man and woman and said "let no man put asunder this pattern. Today, some postmodernists have put asunder God's order and says it's alright for man and man to be married or woman and woman to be partners if they so wish. This is a great evil in the sight of God.

Whenever I look at the animal kingdom, I realize that the so called "lower animals" are more rational than these deviationists. I am yet to see a male dog or female dog having sexual intercourse with their kinds. Even nature teaches us that this is evil. Every animal is intended to respond to the order of the one who created them. In the beginning, God in His infinite wisdom made them "male and female" and not "male and male" or "female and female".

In their research, Sheri and Bob Stritof itemised the right and the wrong reasons why people go into marriage. Bellow is some of the reasons:

Wrong Reasons to Get Married

- Want to be free from parents.
- To have sex.
- To ease loneliness.
- Because of a pregnancy.
- He or she loves you.
- To save or help someone.
- Because you want a baby.
- For money.
- Because all your friends are married.
- You've always wanted a fancy wedding.
- Out of fear that no one else will want to marry you.
- To be happy.
- To be an adult.

Right Reasons to Get Married

- You are in love with one another.
- A desire to share your life with another.
- To have a lifetime companion.
- Realistic expectations.
- Willingness to help one another fulfil their own needs and dreams

A successful marriage is ordained by God, directed by God and protected by Him. If we can truly depart from all our present orientations, mentalities, ideas and beliefs, and internalize in true humility the biblical culture of marriage and family life, then we will be ready to witness a heaven on earth experience in our homes. If it has worked in the past, it can still work in the now. If it has worked for us, I am persuaded it will work for you.

Why Exactly Has God Brought Us Together?

Where the purpose of marriage is misunderstood,
abuse becomes inevitable.

Many people have already written profoundly on this subject. We are familiar with reasons like marriage is for fellowship, for companionship, for fruitfulness, and the rest of them. In as much as I agree with these reasons, let's not see marriage only from human perspective, rather let us view the way God sees marriage. This is the difference between man and the other creatures that also enjoys fellowship, companionship and fruitfulness.

God has a purpose for your home. Before you were born, He has already planned how your home will be, who you shall marry, where you will meet, how you will meet when you will meet, how many children you will have and how He will want your home to look like. This is to say therefore that God has the blue print for your marriage and family life. It amazes me when I see people trying to photocopy the blue print of others in running their home. The truth is that you are not permitted to run your home with the blue print of others. This is not to say that you can not receive godly advice or learn from the successes and failures of others but the secret of success for your home lies with God.

Marriage and family plan was not initiated or originated by man but by God, therefore the purpose of family will be best understood if it is viewed with the lens of God. God will reveal to you the purpose for which He has established your home and the way to achieve that purpose if you truly ask of him. Joy and marital fulfilment starts when we pattern our home in line with God's plans. Bellow is some of the purposes of marriage:

Marriage is a Tool for Exercising Dominion

One of the most important visions in the heart of God for creating the first man—Adam and for joining him in marriage with Eve is so that they will have dominion in His kingdom:

> *"And God said; let us make man in our image, after our likeness:* ***and let them have dominion over the fish of the sea, and over the fowl of the air and over the cattle, and over all the earth, and over every creeping thing that creepeth upon the earth.*** *So God created man in his own image, in the image of God created he him; male and female created he them. And God blessed them, and God said unto them, be fruitful, and multiply, and replenish the earth, and subdue it: and have dominion over the fish of the sea, and over the fowl of the air, and over every living thing that moveth upon the earth."*
> Gen. 1:26-28

The earth was designed by God to be an extension of His kingdom with man as the ruler or ambassador who will faithfully represent him on earth as god—Ps. 82:6. When He made man, He realized that man needed a help meet—an assistant who will labour with him in overcoming all the power of the enemy and effectively take care of His interest on earth. So He initiated marriage in Genesis Chapter two and said to them, *". . . be fruitful, and multiply, and replenish the earth, subdue it: and have dominion over the fish of the sea, and over the fowl of the air, and over every living thing that moveth upon the earth."*

Dominion as mentioned in chapter two means to rule and to reign. It also means a state of unlimited success and victory. God's purpose for marriage is for the husband and wife to team up, put their resources and strength together so that they can reach their desired goal. Marriage is a foundation for greatness. Whatever a person will become is rooted in his foundation. Remember:

> *"Two are better than one; because they have a good reward for their labour, for if they fall, the one will lift up his fellow: but woe to him that is alone when he falleth; for he hath not another to help him up . . ."*
> Eccl.4:9

Marriage is a Channel for Producing Godly Seeds

> *"And did not he make one? Yet had he the residue of the spirit. And wherefore one? **That he might seek a godly seed . . .**" therefore take heed to your spirit, and let none deal treacherously against the wife of his youth. For the Lord, the God of Israel saith that He hateth putting away (divorce): for one covereth violence with his garment, saith the Lord of hosts: therefore take heed to your spirit that you deal not treacherously*
> Mal.2:15-16

The home is intended by God to be a breeding ground for godly children. It is unfortunate that today, we have so many children born out of wedlock; that was not the original plan of God. Children are God's precious gifts to mankind; they should be given the dignity they deserve, nurtured by their legitimate fathers and mothers in a lovely home. This is one of the most important purposes of marriage.

In as much as it is advised that children should not be the determinant of joy, peace or success in the home, the truth still remains that fruitfulness brings additional unity between married couples. The Bible puts it this way:

> *"Lo, children are an heritage of the Lord: and the fruit of the womb is his reward. As arrows are in the hand of a mighty man; so are the children of the youth. Happy is the man that has his quiver full of them: they shall not be ashamed, but they shall speak with the enemies in the gate."*
> Ps.127:3-5

It is not enough to have children, but to bring them up in the proper way as godly seeds, to nurture them to grow in physically and wax strong in the spirit of the Almighty God. The home is rightly qualified by social scientists as the first agent of socialisation.

Marriage is a Channel for Training in Righteousness

Marriage is not just a social institution, it is also a class room where learning is a continuous process and ongoing; no graduation certificate is issued. In marriage, couples are trained not only as partners, but kingdom citizens. In this institution, important courses that are taught and learned are courses like the blessings of patience, the power of endurance, the fruit of forgiveness, the life of faithfulness, the need for trust and the power of love. Others include the lesson of obedience, the place of perseverance, the power of empathy, the need for effective communication and a host of many other practical lessons.

Marital lessons are so important for every couple not minding how long you've been in marriage. The practical lessons that create success in marriage are the same attitude that will take you to heaven. We shall discuss these in details in chapter four.

Marriage is a Channel for Fulfilling Destinies

> *"It's not good for the man to be alone, let's make him a **help meet** . . ."*
> *Gen.2:18*

Marriage is originally ordained by God for achieving divine purpose. In marriage, God brings two souls {man and woman} who He has already destined to shape and support each others destiny. When God gives you a task, He also provides you a wife or a husband who can support you to achieve that assignment. There are some heights you can never get to, some battle you can never win, and some assignment you can not do except through marriage.

There is a popular saying that reads, "Beside every successful man, there is a woman". It should also be noted that beside every successful woman is a man. Marriage is designed for the husband and wife to compliment, encourage and support each other to achieve their God's destined goals in life.

"Yet ye say, wherefore? Because the Lord hath been witness between thee and the wife of thy youth, against whom thou hast dealt treacherously: yet is she thy companion (partner), and the wife of thy covenant"
Mal.2:14

PART TWO

PILLARS OF MARRIAGE

A building without pillars is a great danger to those that dwell within, in the same way every successful marriage needs sustainable pillars.

CHAPTER 4

Things That Makes For Successful Marriage

Marriage Vitamins

". . . What separates happy couples from unhappy couples is not whether they have problems, but how they approach them."
Linda and Robert Miles,

The greatest mistake prospective couples make is over romanticizing every thing about marriage while neglecting the challenges ahead. There are times to weep together and times to laugh together. In the words of Doug Larson "more marriages might survive if the partners realized that sometimes the better comes after the worse." *Garden.com*. If you must succeed in your marriage, you need the under listed factors.

TOLERANCE

"But being happily married means accepting things in your spouse that will never change."
Mavis Leno

"We're a throw-away society, aren't we? We throw away everything. We never even try to fix things—we throw them away, we destroy things—appliances that break, old buildings because they're old, we throw away

> **relationships that aren't exactly what we thought they'd be, we throw away wives, husbands, marriages."**
> *Paul Newman*

I was browsing through a newspaper in my office today when I read the ugly and sad news of one of the foremost world evangelists who according to the paper is facing threat of divorce from his wife for what they termed "irreconcilable difference". At first, I had a shock when I saw it. Then on a second thought, I asked my colleague, "What could be the problem that is irreconcilable if two parties are willing and determine?" for me, **there is no such thing as irreconcilable differences when it has to do with marriage, what we have is unresolved differences.**

Every marital conflict or misunderstanding remains a challenge until it is resolved by two willing, tolerant and determined hearts. A heart of tolerance can go to any extent in resolving marital crises, even if it requires sacrificing your pride and pleasure. **Willingness is the key to every change;** this includes positive changes in the home. Mary Newman writing about her husband says:

> "And he was not easy on himself. He admitted to an earlier, failed marriage, to the usual temptations and near crises that have occurred within his present marriage. But his basic premise was that we must stop throwing things away at the first hint of problems. We must honour the commitments, make an attempt to solve the problem, work at the marriage."

EMPATHY

> *"People always say, 'Work on a marriage.' I think if you work on knowing your own faults and trying to correct them, you're not going to have to work on your marriage."*
> Mavis Leno

Empathy is a strong vitamin for marital bliss. The ability to understand how your spouse might feel by your action or words and work towards positive change defines how empathetic you are. Empathy helps you to acknowledge the opinion and idea of your spouse. A humble man or woman understands that he or she is not complete without the input from the spouse. When you erroneously think that you have it all, then you have no reason to marry at the first place.

Respect each others opinion and show sensitivity to your spouse's feelings. Even the opinion of your children matters, though they might not make complete sense. Empathy does not rudely debunk others' views, but can wisely say, "I sincerely understand what you are saying, but I think it will be better if we . . ." Empathy helps you to feel the plight of others, feel what your spouse is going through and think of the way you can assist. Marriage is not all about celebration, there may be a time to weep together. Feel each others mood and show sincere concern. Elaborating further on this, the Bible puts it thus:

> *"Rejoice with them that do rejoice and*
> *weep with them that weep".*
> Rom.12:15

If God requires us to show empathy for our fellow brethren, then how much more for our family? Empathy at home goes a long way in showcasing your true love, understanding and the care you have for your spouse or family.

PATIENCE

> *"And not only so, but we glory in tribulations also:*
> *knowing that **tribulation worketh patience; and***
> ***patience, experience; and experience, hope"***
> Rom.15:1-4

Words are weapons; they can kill even the liveliest marriage if misused; to be patience is to think before you talk.

Marriage is like an endurance race. Contrary to the popular remarks by zealous counsellors that marriage is to be enjoyed and not to be endured, I want to state that without endurance, enjoyment in marriage will only be a dream. Show me a home that is not willing to patiently tolerate each others weaknesses or imperfection and I will show you a home that is about to hit the rock. Patience is the act of bearing with others' weaknesses, shortcomings and imperfection. It is the grace to endure and persevere in the time of unfavourable circumstances.

The reason for the increase in divorce rate in our society today is as a result of the readiness to break the marriage covenant at any little provocation. The vow "for better for worst" is almost a ceremonial thing in many post modern homes today. Patience is an important ingredient in the recipe for marital success. It takes patience to build your home. A patient husband or wife will treat his or her spouse with respect, knowing that people are different in nature, temperament, intelligence and maturity.

The greatest evil of impatience is that it has the capacity to cause premature death or other health crises that couples go through. The way out of worry and impatience is to prayerfully believe that there is a future gain for the present pain. Don't give up; put your faith in God and in his word. You shall not be disappointed. Remember the old adage that says "slow and steady wins the race", and "a patient dog eats the fattest bone". Every genuinely successful home has a story of patience to tell. Impatience is an emotional thing. Be prepared to take care of your attitude and emotions, gain mastery over your thoughts because like Robert Schuler, "tough time never last but tough people do".

Plain Truth about Patient

- Impatience is a great enemy of marriage
- When you are not patient with your spouse, he or she will lose patience with you.
- Impatient decision, step or action in marriage often gives birth to broken home.
- With patience, pains can be transformed to gain: pain and gain are two sides of a coin, and inseparable.
- No problem is irresolvable between a couple who is determined to be patient with each other and courageous enough to resolve their differences.
- Patience is an important ingredient in the recipe of marital success.

FORGIVENESS

Every relationship requires a price; forgiveness is the price for the growth of any relationship and the healing balm for every marital wound.

Marital wounds are those painful experiences that couples go through in the process of relating with each other. It also includes disgraceful acts of infidelity and unfaithfulness which may cause emotional bruises. These attitudes are never encouraged in marriage. Forgiveness does not favour the offender more than it does to the forgiver. It is the channel to peace of mind to the one that forgives, and peace in the home as well.

Somebody tried defining marriage as the union of two forgiving hearts. The ability to forgive and to overlook past hurts is a healing vitamin for marriage relationship. In addition, it guarantees the physical and emotional wellbeing of the forgiver. There is great wisdom in the words of Roderick C Meredith, *God's Plan for a Happy Marriage* Pg.22 **"we all need to view marriage as a kind of 'workshop' to teach us how to give, how to share and how to forgive others on a continuing basis"**. Forgiveness is not about what I feel like doing, but what I choose to do, the offender may not deserve it, but we are obligated to give it; we never deserve forgiveness from God, yet He gave it to us.

FIDELITY

"If you keep your vows, they will keep your marriage"
Bob Moeller

One of the greatest causes of unfaithfulness in marriage comes from the temptation to compare one's spouse with others. Marriage demands the highest level of responsibility and discipline from couples. Every couple must take responsibility for the decision they made in their choice of marriage partner. Without discipline and faithfulness to your spouse, you can marry 700 wives like Solomon or five husbands like the woman at the well, yet still have problem with unfaithfulness and infidelity. Some people think that marriage is the cure to unfaithfulness, but no! If you are not discipline as a bachelor or spinster you may have problem of infidelity in marriage. Remember that the grass is never greener at the other side; it is the eyes that deceive many.

I remember talking to my cousin some years ago about his promiscuous life style, and he went "Kenn, I find it absolutely difficult to understand how one can cope with one woman". Chyke said in his usual soft tone. He had a serious problem of unfaithfulness when it comes to women. I responded "Chyke, this is why you must give your life to Jesus, he can help you, and the Bible says 'with God, all things are possible" at this time, he laughed, "You know Kenn, variety they said, is the spice of life". This was his shocking reason for promiscuity. Variety of women? Isn't that demonic? Obviously, these words are from the pit of hell. Somebody rightly said that you can choose your goals; you can't choose the consequences. Here is what Honore de Balzac has to say about this.

> "It is as absurd to say that a man can't love one woman all the time as it is to say that a violinist needs several violins to play the same piece of music."

EFFECTIVE COMMUNICATION

Communication is the lifeline of every successful relationship. **A closed mouth is a closed marriage but talking with each other as couples brings reassurance.** Talk about your individual daily experiences; share your feelings, visions, goals and ambitions with each other. The health of every relationship is determined by the effectiveness of the communication between the parties involved. From experience, I have personally discovered that a good marriage is the product of effective communication which is both verbal and non verbal.

What is effective communication in marriage? According to H. Brandit, "communication means to overcome the desire to conceal feelings and thoughts, and to rise to the level of honesty about money, fears, wishes, motivations, sex feelings and responses, mistakes made, resentments and misunderstandings" When couples relate with each other in complete openness, leaving no room for secrets, suspicion and suspense, then they will enjoy effective communication. Effective communicators do not talk at each other, rather they talk with each other; they do not appear uninterested or exhibit boredom during discussion with their spouse. Effective communication requires empathy even when you disagree in your views as couples.

Communication Inhibitors

There are lots of things that inhibit effective communication between couples. These are the things that kill marriages. They include poor listening skills. Some spouses knowingly or unknowingly causes communication breakdown by not showing genuine interest when their spouses engages them in positive discussion. Some are distracted by television, home videos, newspapers and many other factors when discussing with others. All these constitute noise in communication. Another factor that inhibits effective communication between couples is known as "selective retention". Some spouses deliberately choose to retain only the information they like to and forget or rather pretend to forget the information they choose to forget. This is unhealthy for marital relationship.

TRUST

One of the important ingredients in the formula of healthy marital relationship is trust. Trust is an act of possessing unshakable assurance that some one or thing will not fail or disappoint. The pertinent question every spouse must ask is—can my wife trust me? Can my husband trust me? To be trustworthy is to proof beyond doubt that you can not let down or betray the confidence that others (your spouse) have in you. **A broken relationship is a child of a broken trust.**

Where there is trust, disappointment is often maltreated but distrust breeds suspicion. Some years ago when my wife relocated to England, I stayed behind in Nigeria with the hope of joining her soonest. What seems like just a short while latter turned out to be over four years. Within those years, we had and heard all sorts of discouraging nonsense called advice and gossips. One thing we never forsook was trust. When we spoke with each other, we kept reaffirming our trust in each other and this helped us to remain faithful knowing that it is callousness to break a heart that trusts you.

One of the secret of building trust in marital relationship starts from your life style and behaviour towards each other during courtship. **If you are giving in to sex before marriage just because you are put under pressure by your partner, you are sowing seeds that will destroy future trust in that relationship.** When you are married, your minds will continue to play games with you; you will still see each other as that weak fellow that will always compromise when put under pressure. You will be struggling with the belief that your spouse might just give in when pressurized by others. This is the root of distrust.

A Pastor friend told me about a case of a couple that invited him to settle a prolonged marriage crisis between them. When he listened to each of them narrate their stories, he realised that both are victims of acute case of prolonged marital distrust. They falsely accused each other of flirting. When the Pastor engaged them in further counselling, the man lamented, "Pastor, my wife can not stay without a man cuddling her, when we were courting, she never gave me rest so how can she convince me that while I travelled, she was . . ." Before he finished, the wife rudely interrupted, "Pastor, don't listen to this cheat, while we were in courtship, he was the one that kept putting me under pressure, he kept pressurising me to sleep with him, this is why I said that my husband cannot discipline himself when he travels". This is a genuine case of distrust which originated from indiscipline during courtship. May God help us.

The greatest tragedy in relationship is to fall in love with some one you can not trust. It's better to be alone than to marry someone you can not trust. Trust is difficult to build, but often quite easy to destroy. When you keep lying to your spouse, living a life of secrecy and suspicious relationship with the opposite sex, you are sowing seed for distrust. Don't give your spouse reason to distrust you.

RESPECT

Giants stoop to conquer

The greatest error in marriage is the belief by couples that standing is a proof of strength while stooping is a sign of weakness; on the contrary, the true proof of strength is the possession of the knowledge of when to stoop.

This is the proof of wisdom and respect. For me, giants in marriage are those who conquered their marital challenges by stooping.

Respect for one's spouse is one of the greatest virtues in marriage. Being courteous requires respect for each other. Remember to say "please" and "thank you". Remember also to keep your promises to each other as well as important days. If you have respect for your spouse, you will treat him as you would a stranger you want to impress. Don't develop the habit of badmouthing your spouse to your friends, relations or associates; it is a sign of disrespect. **To disrespect your spouse is a proof that you have no respect for your self.**

Respect for each other is the bedrock of every successful marriage. Mutual respect in marriage is evident in the way we talk to our spouse, the way we act and react towards each other. This is one of the most important ingredients that make a healthy marriage.

INTIMACY

"Intimacy is not a formula; it is a way of life."
Diana Hagee

Understanding your spouse breeds marital agreement and intimacy. Intimacy is the unfailing key to fruitful relationship. Show me a home where there is no intimacy and I will show you the home that can not withstand a storm. The reason things go wrong in relationship is the absence of intimacy. When we spend less time together with our spouse, we are laying a strong foundation for marital collapse. This is because the image of God in man is the image that craves after love and intimacy.

Intimacy is the absence of secrets in relationship, to be absolutely naked. It is love expressed; secret love does not grow relationship. Intimacy is not automatic; it is developed, nurtured and enjoyed by two selfless hearts.

APPRECIATION

Do you express sincere appreciation to your spouse or do you consider every kind deed from your spouse as a right? Spouses need to be thanked. They need to know they are appreciated. The words "thank you" goes a long way to show how much you appreciate and value each other. If you have nothing to appreciate your spouse for, thank him or her for marrying you.

Give your spouse a sense of significance by appreciating and valuing them. This is different from flattering; don't flatter, be real. Somebody may ask, "what if there is nothing to appreciate him or her for?" Even when your spouse performs below the expectations you have of them, give them confidence and let him or her know that you have hope in their ability to change or recover.

There is always something good in every one, concentrate on your spouse's strong virtues and deflate the weaknesses. Remember those things which attracted you to your spouse at the initial. No one is completely bad just as you might not be completely good. The two words—"thank you" may just be all you need to turn your relationship around. Every one loves appreciation, including God. Appreciation some times might also require you to spend some cash, buy something that your spouse values just to tell him or her that this is your own way of saying thank you for marrying me.

APOLOGY

Film Erich Segalin in his classic movie "Love Story", a best selling novel award winning says "love means never having to say I am sorry". As interesting and thought provoking as this may sound, I realize that love means the opposite. For me, love means saying I am sorry over and over again with a genuine intention not to insult the privilege of forgiveness. The only proof we can show that we love God and others is to say I am sorry when we fall short of their expectation. To refuse to apologise to some one you love is to take love for granted and your relationship may never get to the peak of its fulfilment until you learn to apologize.

Apology does not depreciate respect, dignity and self worth; on the contrary, it makes you more dignified, respected and responsible. Amanda Craig's novel "Hearts and Minds" reads, "real love is about the give and take of sorry—but until couples realise this, they can't move forward".

Pride is the enemy of apology, it is the poison which eats deep into many relationships, marriages and families and robs couples the gracious tendency of saying I am sorry when wrong. It doesn't matter if you've made an insignificant mistake or a great mistake, what matters is that you need to accept the responsibility for that mistake, accept it, apologize for it, fix it if you can, and do not repeat it.

SACRIFICE OR GIVING

The path to marital bliss requires sacrifice; the responsibility to turn your marriage "for better" or "for worse" is yours.

Stability and fulfilment in marriage is costly but it worth the cost. No marriage thrives without commitment and sacrifice from both spouses. Marriage will require you as a man to sacrifice your time and sometime even your company with friends just to make your darling wife happy. There is nothing that is too much to forsake so as to have peace and joy in your home.

The heart of a good husband or wife is the one that is willing to give selflessly and not the one that is always willing to receive: give your love, give your respect, give your service, give your resources and give your all. Some men are so stingy even to their wives. The same men are ready to spend their last penny on outsiders, choosing rather to impress others while their family remains in misery. This camouflage and self centred life style is a recipe for crisis.

Until a woman is ready to sacrifice her pride and be ready to submit to her husband, she should remain single. The greatest reason for divorce today is the struggle for "rights". In a home where no one is ready to sacrifice his or her rights for the unity and progress of the home, then stability becomes only an illusion. **The greatest gift a man can give to his wife is not money, but his heart.**

CHAPTER 5

When the Heart Beat Is One

The power of marital agreement

"Can two walk together, except they be agreed?"
Amos3:3

The reason for the cut in and cut out we have in marriages today goes a long way to show that many couple are far from the knowledge of the truth of marriage as a covenant or an agreement.

*"Yet ye say, wherefore? Because the Lord hath been witness between thee and the wife of thy youth, against whom thou hast dealt treacherously: yet is she thy companion, and **the wife of thy covenant**."*
Mal.2:14

Every covenant or agreement has conditions, obligations and price. The price of marriage is sacrifice and selflessness. The Almighty God who is the initiator of marriage is a God of covenant, He knows that there is power in agreement and that was why He created the woman to be an help to the man in planning, working and achieving their destinies together. In Eccl.4:9, the Scripture records:

"Two are better than one; because they have a good reward for their labour, for if they fall, the one will lift up his fellow: but woe to him that is alone when he falleth; for

> **he hath not another to help him up. Again, if two lie together, then they have heat: but how can one be warm alone? And if one prevails against him, two shall withstand him; and a three fold cord is not quickly broken."**

MARITAL MATHS

Do You Share The Same Heartbeat?

Marriage is the only union that defies the principle of arithmetical correctness of 1 + 1 = 2. In "marital maths", 1 + 1 = 1.

> *"Therefore shall a man leave his father and his mother, and shall cleave unto to his wife and they shall be one flesh."*
> Gen.2:24

This goes a long way to depict the power of marital agreement. In marriage, God makes two hearts to beat as one by divine blending.

The power of agreement was further illustrated in Genesis 11:5:

> *"And the Lord came down to see the city and the tower, which the children of men builded. And the Lord said behold, the people is one, and they have all one language; and this they begin to do: **and now nothing will be restrained from them, which they have imagined to do.**"*

In the above scripture, the people have a vision to build a tower whose "top may reach unto heaven"; this was the old Tower of Babel. They almost succeeded in building the great tower until the Lord impeded their progress by confusing their language and breaking their agreement. The lesson here is that if people who do not have any divine backup can make such agreement and almost succeeded, then nothing shall be impossible for a couple whose heart is one in prayers, planning, preparation, programming and pursuit of purpose. This is why Satan labours day and night to cause disagreement and disaffection in homes. He knows that a home where there is agreement can never be hindered from their breakthrough. You shall hit the tower of your marital dreams from today.

Disagreement in marriage is the crack through which marital blessings leaks out of the home. A home where there is no agreement between the couple is only a house. When I see some husbands transacting business, making and spending money, taking some major decisions and investments about the future without carrying their wives along, it makes me to wonder the level of respect they have for their wives. Sometimes you hear them saying to their wives, "it's never your business whatever I do with my life or my money or even my time". This is an abuse of marriage and that is why such ventures done without spousal agreement often do not succeed.

Women on the other hand need to show genuine interest in the success of their husband's vision. Always remember that God brought you to that man to help him succeed and not to build your own empire or to be a success saboteur. I was in a seminar where I was teaching about the fruit of unity in marriage and how couples can make financial plans and savings. After the session, a man met me and said, "Sir, if only you know the kind of wife I have, you would not have recommended that I should do financial plan with her, the day she knows how much I have in my account, I will become bankrupt the next day". This is marital sabotage and not a good testimony for a virtues wife. If this is your story, please change. Submission requires a wife to pursue her dreams and aspirations under the umbrella and the agreement of her husband.

> *It takes a united couple to give birth to united children and they all work together to make a united home.*

A LESSON FROM THE TRINITY

> *"That they all may be one; as thou, father, art in me, and I in thee that they also may be one in us . . ."*
> Jn.17:21

One of the biggest lessons of agreement in the home is that illustrated by the trinity. The Unity of purpose, bond of fellowship and mutual agreement between the Father, Son and Holy Spirit is a clear pointer to what God intends the home to be. In trinity, three became one; in marriage, two became one and where the union is blessed with children, the third party is formed. It is a reflection of God's oneness. This is why divorce is not acceptable in marriage. There is no separation between the God head. Did I hear you say—but we're not God? Read Ps.82:6,

It is expected that the harmony enjoyed by the trinity should be reflected in our homes between husbands, wives and children as well. Plans and decision should be made in consultation and agreement with every member of the family. This inseparable bond is what makes us unique and different from other creatures.

THE THREE LEGGED RACE

Another strong analogy that perfectly teaches what agreement in marriage is all about is the three legged race. As I looked through the window of the class room of one of the schools I worked with some years ago, I got carried away watching some pupils as they practised for their forth coming inter house sports. One of the sports they practised was "three legged race". In this race, two people stand side by side each other with one's right leg tied to the other's left leg. The partners are expected to walk simultaneously with their legs moving together and any effort to leave the other behind could lead to a great fall. As I watched keenly while the children moved with the left leg and the right leg moving together, the reality of Amos 3:3 became clearer to me. *Can two walk together, except they be agreed?"*

Marriage is not the union of two perfect hearts; rather it is the union of two tolerant hearts that have agreed to beat as one. The simultaneous movement of the right and left legs showcases patience, tolerance and agreement. This teaches that a husband must not leave his wife behind in decisions and actions needed to move the home forward. Any attempt by one of the couple to leave the other behind can lead to marriage failure. **The home should be a place of complimentary gifts and not a place of competition. What is lacking in the man may be housed in the wife, and what is absent in the parents may be found in their children.**

CHAPTER 6

Your Wife Needs a Husband

Understanding your role as a husband

Your wife needs a husband and not a boss. One of the major reasons why some marriages hit the rock is as a result of husbands playing the role of the boss in the home instead of the role of a husband. The home requires a leader and not a boss. So many husbands are dictators; they oppose and deal mercilessly with any sign of dissatisfaction and unconformity from their wives. Their words are often regarded as the last order which must never be challenged or contravened. They show little or no patience for advice and opinion from their wives. If you happened to be in this category, then you should be in the barracks commanding armed forces. **Your home is not a barracks.** This is what I termed the five P roles of a husband in the home.

THE FIVE P ROLES OF A HUSBAND

This is a **Christ—church model** of relationship. The principal role of a husband to his wife is to **love** and to **care. Loving your wife is not conditional.** Some time ago, there was an issue between my wife and I, when we settled it, she looked at me and asked "honey do you still love me?" then the Spirit of God said to me **"loving your wife is not an option; it is a compulsory and an unconditional decision."** He said to me, **"the day you stop loving your body, then you can stop loving your wife. This is because your wife is your body."** After that, I told my wife that there is no need asking that question because; she already knows what my answer will be.

> **"True love does not wither or die. It merely ripens.'"**
> Rev. Susanna Stefanachi Macomb.

Don't give your wife any condition for loving her. Some men will often say "how can I love you when you are not submissive to me?" The Bible says that *"while we were yet sinners, Christ died for us."* We were rebellious to our creator, our maker and head Jesus Christ, yet He loved us and died for us. Below are the five p roles of a husband.

A Provider

In the Christ—Church model, Jesus Christ selflessly gave himself to the church. The greatest gift a man can give to his wife is the gift of himself—a selfless giving of his heart to his wife. A true husband derives pleasure by providing for his family. It is rather a shame for the man to fold his hands and expect his wife to assume the position of the bread winner of the home. The Bible puts it this way:

> *"But if any provide not for his own, and specially for those of his own house, he has denied the faith, and is worse than an infidel"*
> *1 Tim.5:8*

Should we now recommend that if a man is genuinely incapacitated or unavoidably constrained by finance, that he should lose his respect in the home? No! Nevertheless, every man should trust God for the grace to take care of the needs of his wife and children. You must not be a millionaire to do this, remember, little things matters.

A Protector

It is the duty of the man to protect his wife physically, spiritually and in every other area of life where she needs his covering just as Christ protects his body, which is the church. A husband is like a canopy for his wife to shield her from the rain, sun or storm of life. He needs divine assistance to be able to adequately fit into this role. The man and his wife both need security from their maker. It is only when a man is secured that he can give security to others. In the words of Mary Stewart:

> *". . . There can be no happy and healthy marriage until the individual partner is happy and secure . . . It is only when the individual is secure in his own identity and self-worth that he can contribute to the marriage in a healthy, non-degenerative way."*
> Mary Stewart

Women need protection from unfriendly in-laws. A friend once told me a story of a friend of his who was visited by his mother. After his mother left, that home never remained the same again. The first shock his wife experienced was that on the arrival of her mother in-law, her husband instructed her to start sleeping on the floor of their one bed apartment, while his mother sleeps on the bed with him. When she protested, she was beaten mercilessly by her husband while her mother in-law watches. What a shame.

A Promoter

A popular saying has it that if you don't blow your trumpet, nobody will blow it for you. When a man promotes his wife, he is promoting himself but to demote your wife is to demote yourself. You don't gain respect by damaging the image and character of your wife before others. When a woman realizes that you are ready to cover her nakedness before others most especially before relations despite her many weaknesses, that woman will be ready to treat you as a king.

It is the duty of a man to lift his wife to the level he desires her to be. I have seen men who divorced their wives simply because they feel that she has suddenly become inferior to them, they have acquired one degree or the other which now makes them despise their wives and to look for alternatives. Such men often never have peace for the rest of their lives. Don't give others the privilege to insult your wife because of your treatment to her.

A Producer

A husband is a producer. To be productive is to be fruitful. When God created Adam, the first instruction to Adam in Gen.1:28 was ". . . be fruitful (productive) . . ." God desires the man to be fruitful biologically through deep relationship with his wife. It is the responsibility of the man and his wife to produce their kind.

Productivity is not only biological, it's not all about producing children, but also achieving results. A husband is expected to be a hard worker. **A lazy man is a disgrace to his household.** The man should have a clear vision about the purpose of God for the family and should successfully interpret it to his wife. He should motivate and encourage his wife to pursue the family vision and aspiration with him.

A Man of Prayer

The challenges facing many homes today is that we have more antagonising men than we have interceding men. I think our homes will be a heaven on earth if we can spend just a little of the time spend arguing and quarrelling to pray for our spouse. A praying man is a victorious man. Being physically forceful and violent is less fruitful in marriage than being prayerful.

In the Christ—church model of the home, the greatest work that Christ does for the church is the work of intercession. This is because anointing the Bible says flows from the head. Since the man is the head of his wife—1Cor.11:3 "The head of the woman is the man . . ." It is his responsibility to let the anointing flow from him to his wife. It is unquestionably true that God has regard for spousal prayers most especially when it comes from the head of the woman.

Your wife needs your prayers. Pray for her fruitfulness, pray for her health, pray for every aspect of her life most especially the aspect of her life that makes you uncomfortable.

CHAPTER 7

Your Husband Needs a Wife

The role of wives to their husbands

Women are born; wives are made

Your husband needs a wife not just a woman, there are many women all over the place, yet the Bible was vocal to say *"he that finds a wife finds a better thing and obtaineth favour from the Lord"* A woman who has the fear of God is the greatest marriage gift from God. She gives her husband a lift in all life's ramifications. *"Favour is deceitful, and beauty is vain: but **a woman that feareth the Lord, she shall be praised"** Prov. 31:30.* **Don't be deceived or carried away by favour or gifts; seek God's face for your life partner.**

THE MAKING OF A MODEL WIFE

As I sat pondering why some women are happily married to men of their dreams and children who they can be proud of while others are either having difficulty getting married or found themselves in a turbulent marriage, I got a shocking answer: **Women are born; wives are made.** I must emphasize that it is not in all cases that turbulent home is as a result of women's poor attitude but the truth remains that the difference between "a woman" and "a wives" is in their virtues. Women become wives when their virtues become nurtured. What makes a woman a wife and mother is not the ability to find a husband or to give birth to a child, but the wisdom to build and manage the home. Some of the qualities that make a good wife is summarised in what I termed the 5S of a wife.

THE 5 "S" ROLE OF A WIFE

Here, we are going to work by the **church—Christ model** of relationship where a wife performs her duty to her head who is her husband just as the body of Christ {the church} relates with her head who is Jesus Christ. This order is not intended by any means to make the woman inferior to a man, rather it is a unique way of making her fulfilled and flourishing in her God's giving position. The 5s role of the husband includes:

She Supports

*"And the Lord God said it is not good that the man should be alone; I will make him an **help meet** for him".*
Gen. 2:18

God designed the woman to be a help meet for her husband. The Hebrew word for help meet means a suitable assistant, the help could be physical help, intellectual help, spiritual help, moral help and every other help they need to perform their God giving responsibility. A helper is a supporter, a pillar and a counterpart. A true wife is a co labourer with her husband in the pursuit of their destiny; she is a reliable supporter and an unflinching believer in her husband's God giving vision.

A good wife should not be a saboteur to the success of her home. Eve was a big disappointment to her maker when she turned out to be a destiny killer instead of a destiny builder; she received a curse for that. God brought you to your husband so that you can be a blessing to him and not a curse. Give him the help and assistance he requires. God has placed in you all that is lacking in your husband for a strong support.

She Submits

"Wives, submit yourselves unto your own husbands, as unto the Lord. For the husband is the head of the wife, even as Christ is the head of the church: and he is the saviour of the body. Therefore as the church is subject unto Christ, so let the wives be to their own husbands in everything."
Eph. 5:22-24

Submission is not humiliation, it brings respect and not insult, it is not inferiority but humility, and it doesn't make you subservient but a celebrity. It brings out the godly quality that characterizes a spirit filled daughter of God. Your submission to your husband is not conditional. I often hear women say "if he doesn't love me enough or care for me, why should I submit? The body of Christ which we are does not and can not give Christ any condition for submitting to His authority.

An attitude of submission from a humble wife can change even the most arrogant and difficult husband. It is possible that you are wealthier than your husband, more influential than him, older than him; more educated than him, yet God has tied your blessing and fruitfulness to your submission to him. Be wise.

She Sacrifices

It is not an abomination for a woman to be wealthier, more prominent or academically higher than her husband, but it is an abomination in the sight of God if she can not sacrifice her pride and humble her self before her husband. A wife must deny herself of her ego if she genuinely desires to be what God has ordained her to be and to receive the blessings God has kept in stock for her in marriage.

No woman is honoured for what she received from her husband, but for what she sacrificed for him. Read this:

> *"A virtuous woman is a crown to her husband: but she that maketh ashamed is as rottenness in his bones."*
> Prov. 12:4

Sacrifice demands you praying for your husband and planning with him. It will cost you your time, resources and maybe other precious things. Any sacrifice you make for your husband is a sacrifice for yourself. **The disappointing truth is that sometimes your husband might not appreciate or value what you do for him, never give up. Your sacrifice will speak for you some day.**

She Supplements

*"Whoso findeth a wife findeth a good thing,
and obtaineth favour of the LORD"*
Prov.18:22

The best word for this is a life partner or a trustworthy counterpart. **A man is not yet complete except he finds his life partner.** This goes a long way to explain the irreplaceable role of a woman in the home. On several occasions, I have been invited to some events; while I am busy preparing, it may never occur to me that certain things are needed to be purchased either as gifts or presents, but I will be surprise to discover that my wife has purchased and prepared all the necessary things. On such occasions, I will always remember that I am incomplete without her.

God designed the wife to complement what is lacking in the husband. A balanced home is often a union of two people with unique temperaments complementing each other. The work of food supplement is to release some vitamins into the body system to make up for those lacking from the food we eat. **A complimentary wife is like a vitamin that supplement what is lacking in her husband. She is a blessing from the lord.**

She Serves

Darrell L. Hines was right when he said that "every wife is a minister" *Resolving Conflict in Marriage, Pg 37*. Every wife is ordained by God to be a minister. She is not a good servant of God until she learns to serve the man that God has placed to be her head and her glory. **A wise woman knows that when she stoops for her husband she conquers him. When you make your husband feel like a king, he treats you like a queen.** Prov 31:11-24 says:

> *"The heart of her husband doth safely trust in her, so that he shall have no need of spoil. She will do him good and not evil all the days of her life . . . she is not afraid of the snow for her household: for all her household are clothed with scarlet . . . her husband is known in the gates, when he sitteth among the elders of the land."*

I strongly believe that if we have more serving women as we have nagging women, our homes will be a lovely place to live. Some women will rather give their respect and services to their boss in office, friends and colleagues, but at home they insult, fight and usurp the authority of their husbands. This is hypocrisy. Your boss could only give you temporary promotion, but your husband occupies a divine position to place blessing or curse upon you. If I were you I will choose to serve him as unto the Lord, others may tell you that you are timid by ministering or serving your husband, but wisdom will tell you that virtuous women conquer through obedience.

PART THREE

BUILDING YOUR HOME ACCORDING TO PATTERN

A man without goal is a football in the field of destiny, used by others to achieve their goals.

CHAPTER 8

Planning For Your Home

The Place of Planning

"The preparation of the heart in man, and the answer of the tongue, is from the Lord. All the ways of a man are clean in his own eyes; but the Lord weigheth the spirits. Commit thy works unto the Lord, and thy thoughts shall be established.
Prov.16:1-3

If you have no plan for your home, Satan does. It is the responsibility of couples to discover, plan and carry out God led plans for their home. **Two things, men plan for their home using the blue print of God, God directs their steps. Planning gives your life or your home direction.** As a learner driver or a traveller, you must have been told that the way to minimise stress and time loss on your journey is by planning your route ahead. The same applies to your journey of destiny, most especially the journey to marital fulfilment.

There is no such thing as an "already made" home; a successful home is a product of learned principles, planning, discipline, nurturing and determination to succeed. **The ability to be a good husband, wife, father or mother does not come by nature but by nurture,** it is not a natural experience but a nurtured experience. It is possible that God might have spoken to you in a very thunderous voice that a particular sister is your wife or a particular brother is your husband; the truth is that **God's**

voice alone does not build home, but God's wisdom, knowledge and understanding. This is where planning, discipline and prayers comes in.

A successful home is a blessing from God but places a demand on us for nurturing. The responsibility of becoming a good couple or wonderful parents is not God's but men. The fact that your family is going through a stormy period presently or your marriage may be at the point of collapse is not a proof that God is not in that home, but it is a proof that you have need of wisdom that will help nurture your home. This book is God's answer to that problem in Jesus name.

> *"For I know the thoughts {plans} that I think toward you, saith the Lord, thoughts of peace, and not of evil, to give you an expected end."*
> *Jer.29:11*

Whose model do you follow in planning for your home? **There are two factors that play major role in shaping every home: the word of God and the world around us.** God is a perfect planner but so many people run their home with the pattern prescribed by their culture and tradition without questioning or assessing the effectiveness of such practice.

Every home is a distinct entity in God's agenda having its own challenges and driven by Goals

A goalless home is an unfruitful home. It is expected of every home to have goals. Your goal as a family is that purpose for which you are brought together. What is your home living for? Somebody said that a man without plan will spend his life solving other people's plans. We can as well conclude **that a family without goal will be a foot ball in the field of destiny. Others will play and shoot you around just to hit their own goal.** To leave in a goalless home is a life of tragedy; such home is a breeding ground for failures and mediocre.

Planning and executing goals together is the pillar behind the strength of every home. It helps to foster peace, joy and oneness in the home. When your spouse is involved in your plans, the goal becomes "our goal" and not "his or her goal". It is one thing to have a goal, and another thing to properly interpret it to your family. Every member of your family should know what your home is set up for. Try as much as possible to communicate and inculcate your goals and vision to your children, and let them "run with it". Effective family goals include plan for family health, plan for family investment, family trips, and children academic programmes; above all, plan for spiritual development.

EVERY CHILD MATHERS

The family has been classified by sociologists as the first agent of socialization. What ever a child will be in life is rooted in his or her family upbringing. There have been divergent views and opinions among scholars concerning the most effective model for child upbringing. While some favour the authoritarian model where rules and regulations take pre-eminence over relationship, and parents-child communication is minimal with little or no intimacy. Others support the permissive model where self esteem is highly encouraged with minimal or no discipline for the child.

The limitations of the two models is that while authoritarian model nurtures children who grow up to be timid and naive always wanting to please others and lack the ability to take initiative, the permissive model raises children who grow up without self control and restraint, always insisting on their ways with little tolerance for others. A combination of the two models produces a "relational authority", which is what the child needs for a balanced growth and development. In such homes, children enjoy good relationship and communication with their parents who encourage them and direct them on the right terrain of life. Here, kingdom driven rules are made to neutralize the onslaught of satanic lifestyle of this post modern age.

Children should be given the liberty to ask why or why not and parents are obligated to furnish them with the right answers. This is what makes a "proper child". A proper child should also be allowed to make mistakes. Mistake plays an important role in the development of a child. This is because there is something a child can learn from every mistake.

Kenn Mark

THE PROPER CHILD

> *"By faith Moses, when he was born, was hid three months of his parents, because they saw he was **a proper child**, and they were not afraid of the king's commandment"*
> Heb.11:23

I was about to graduate from the university when the news of the death of my childhood and closest friend got to me. On hearing this ugly news, I quickly took off as fast as I could to his house to confirm the truth of the news. When I got to his house, I saw people gathered in groups outside the house with tears rolling down their cheeks while others cried aloud. Without any further evidence, I immediately knew that the information was true. "Where is Daddy {that was the name I called my friend's father)? I asked his younger sister who could not be consoled. I was directed into the room where I met with Daddy. At this point, I could no more hold it, so I let the tears flow freely. On seeing me, Daddy came to me, and as we held each other; he made a statement which has re-echoed in my ears till today. He said, while trying helplessly to hold his tears "Kenn, I've lost a proper son".

One will be surprise why he made this statement knowing that my friend was not the only son of his father, yet he called him a proper son. But your surprise would have been over when I tell you that the only son left after the death of my friend was so irresponsible, he was a problem to his family and he never gave peace to the community as well till he was shot dead in arm robbery offence.

Moses' parents hid him for three months because they realise (I don't know how, but perhaps by divine or prophetic insight) that he was a proper child—goodly, godly and beautiful. One thing pertinent in the story of Moses is that it takes a proper parent to raise a proper child. Moses would have died like an ordinary child in Pharaoh's hand if they had not taken a precarious initiative to the extent of putting their lives on the line, to guarantee Moses his safety.

Moses' mother was not afraid to inculcate into her son the most important phrase that shaped his destiny, "you are not an Egyptian". We can not under estimate the impact we can make in our children if we can always emphasize to them—you are not a failure, you are not a mediocre, you are not a gay, you are not a lesbian, you are not an atheist, you are not an infidel, a drunker, smoker, or any other negative identity that the society might choose for them. **If you love your child, bring him up in a proper way. A proper child brought up in an improper way becomes two times an improper child.**

Good parenting requires respect for the child's individualism, personality and diversity while guiding them on the path to their divine destiny. Parenting is one of the greatest challenges confronting the post-modern family. This is because of the upsurge of ungodliness which has pervaded the society around us: what our children are made to belief at school, what they hear and see on the television, what they browse on the internet, what they learn from their peers and all other negative influences. The role of parents in the upbringing, nurturing and mentoring of their children is a very demanding task. Your children don't need any other person to play the role of daddy or mummy. No body else can best perform that role no matter how close, nice or caring they are but you.

The reason for low performance in child training today is, because many parents are using the strategy our fathers used in the pre-modern and modern era to solve the challenges of the post-modern age. We must accept the reality that time has changed, and according to Edmond Burke, "the law of change is the most powerful law of nature". We must devise a means of making the Christian culture relevant to our children lest we lose them. This is not to say that we should dilute the truth of God's word in an attempt to make it relevant to the post modern child.

What we can do is to change or rather enhance our style of communicating and relating with our children. Our discipline and correction technique must also be improved on. The old authoritarian style must be replaced with relative authority(be firm yet develop a good parent-child rapport) Today's children need parents who are role models, parents who show genuine interest in the affaires of their children and encourage self esteem.

Effective child training demands respect for the child's different gifting and talents while encouraging the development of their personality in line with clear understanding of God's expectation for them. Your children are not your personal property, you never made them as some people proclaim in absolute ignorance—"let's make children." The only maker of all things including your children is the Almighty God.

> "Lo children are an heritage of the Lord: and
> the fruit of the womb is his reward".
> Ps.127:3

Children are God's precious gift to us; they should be loved, cared for, planned for and be treated as the kings children.

Plans for Their Welfare

A discouraged child is a rebellious child. Children need reassurance of our love for them. When children are denied the parental love they crave for, they become unavoidably attracted to the assurances and false promises of love provided by friends. Your children need focused attention. According to Rose Campbell in her book "How to Really Love Your Teenager" P. 31, "focussed attention means giving your teenager(or toddler) full, undivided attention in such a way that he feels truly loved, that he knows he is valuable in his own right, that he warrants your watchfulness, appreciation, and uncompromising regard".

> "Fathers provoke not your children to
> anger lest they be discouraged"
> Col.3:21

Plan for Their Future

> "For I know the thoughts(plans) that I think
> towards you, saith the Lord, thoughts of peace, and
> not of evil, to give you an expected end."
> Jer.29:11

If you don't give your children a solid plan for their future, they will grow to become victims of others' plan. What are you doing to safe guide the future of your children? Proper parents are the ones that are not short sighted rather they have good vision about the future of their children and plan towards it. It is your responsibility to train up your child spiritually, morally, academically, psychologically and in every other aspect of life so that they become a blessing to the society and not a minus. To successfully do this, you need to ride on the help of God. Pray for strength, wisdom, knowledge and the understanding required to nurture the precious gifts He has given you.

Two things, if you are not planning for the future of your child, you have inevitably planned for their failure. Do you have any financial plans for your child's future? Do you make any savings or investment in their name? What are your plans for their education? The emphasis here is that you are the significant person as far as your child's future is concerned. May God give you the grace. Parents who fail to plan for the future of their children have already made plans for their children's failure.

Plan for Their Eternity

Some times it appears as though some parents are under some dose of spiritual anaesthetics that has doused their feelings and makes them insensitive to the decay of this "perilous time". You are not doing your child a favour by permitting him or her to always do things their own way without restraint. Many parents today are lost in the same sin of Eli {1Sam.2}. When you deny your children the right discipline they require, you are paving way for the birth of Icabod (The glory of God has departed)

Parents should consider child training as a divine assignment and stop being selfish in the manner in which they handle their children. Don't shape them to become what you want them to be, rather train them to become what God wants them to be. **A "proper child" is not a product of nature but nurture.** It is our role as parents to continuously neutralize the garbage dumped in the mindsets of our children through television, peer group influence, schools and other agents that play important roles in shaping their minds.

You will be amazed to discover that the present day children know more about evolution theory than they know about the biblical creation story. In his book "Lord, Why Is My Child a Rebel?" Jacob Aranza asked a very pertinent question, "Do you want to know the most bitter, resentful children I've ever met? The kids whose mothers and fathers failed to provide guidelines and discipline, children who live in permissive homes have trouble believing their parents really care about them". (P.45)

Your child should know that there is a penalty attached to every pervasion. It is not love to tell them that it is well when every attitude they exhibit shows that there is danger if nothing is done urgently.

> *"The rod and reproof give wisdom: but a child left to himself bringeth his mother to shame . . . correct thy son and he shall give thee rest; yea, he shall give delight unto thy soul."*
> *Prov. 29:15-17*

CHAPTER 9

Ingredients of Good Parenting

*Don't just pray for your child to be godly,
show him how to be godly.*

An article was written by Tola Onigbanjo in the Voice newspaper of 26th March, 2010 on the topic "Seven Biggest Mistakes Parents Make". The parenting expert outlined seven important points every parent must avoid. From her research, she discovered that children are worried because:

- Parents don't understand them
- Parents don't spend much time with their children
- Parents don't teach their children values; they teach opinion
- They do not give boundaries
- They expose children too much
- They don't give enough praise
- They always compare their children with others.

Parenting a child is like preparing a meal, the right application of the ingredients is a recipe for a delicious outcome. Parents must go the extra mile in understanding their children. Some children are more complex to understand than others because of their nature, but parents must not give up. You are obligated to know the strength and weaknesses of your child listen to their questions and worries and explain why they should do or do not some things. You can not understand your children until you start spending time with them. This is when you will discover their nature and characters, strength and weaknesses. Parents should get into the life of their children, learn the things that interest them, take them out for leisure and play games with them.

It is important your child knows your values and your beliefs. Some children are leaving in confusion because their parents are living in deceit and double standard lifestyle. Children don't just want to know your opinion, but your conviction and lifestyle. They should not be confused about what their parents can condone and what they will disallow. Children who know their boundaries are more discipline than the ones that are left in the valley of trial and error.

I have discovered that parents who spend more time in praising and rewarding their children's good behaviour and performance creates more room for better performance than those who spend ages nagging over every mistake or poor attitude of the child. I am not discouraging correction and reproof from parents, but deliberate downplaying of some errors while highlighting and rewarding good behaviour could be a more fruitful way of instilling positive character change in the child. Children grow up with negative self image or inferiority complex when they are often compared with others who may "appear" to be doing better than them. This is an error from parents. Every child has his self esteem, no child is completely the same, even if they are twins; they have different destinies.

YOUR CHILD NEEDS A MODEL

> "Therefore shall you lay up these my words in your hearts and in your soul, and bind them for a sign upon your hand, that they may be as frontlets between your eyes. AND **you shall teach them your children**, speaking of them when thou sittest in thy house, and when thou walkest by the way, and when thy liest down, and when thou risest up."
> Deut.11:18-19

The greatest challenge facing Christian parents today is how to make our Christian culture relevant to the post-modern home. The impact of the present day cultural shift has eroded the traditional Christian belief, thereby leaving us with a generation of children trying very hard to balance what they hear their parents say and what they see in the society where they live. The Bible records:

> *"Train up a child in the way he should go and*
> *when he grows he shall not depart from it".*
> *Prov. 22:6*

The post modern world is a world of diverse choices and decisions, which may not necessarily be rational. I have a strong persuasion that if our children are not only taught the right things, but also shown a model of the right path through our conversations and character, it will be an effective tool for decision making when the need arises. Somebody once said "if you are very familiar with truth, when you see a lie, you will know".

Effective child training is not all about what you taught the child, but what you demonstrated to the child, it is not about what the child heard you say, but what the child saw you do. It is possible for a child to forget what they hear or what they are taught, but rarely will a child forget what he or she saw mummy and daddy do. The old adage "do as I say but not as I do" is no more relevant in this present age. If we must navigate our family through the terrain of this amoral age while still making Christ the focal point of our doctrine, then self development and discipline becomes an unavoidable pursuit.

I remember the little lies my aunt taught us to tell those days. She lived with my parents as our carer. She was so caring and loving that we literally grew up to be too attached to her. All the same, she had her challenges. One of the challenges she faced then was how to handle the influx of male friends perambulating our house like rams running after the sheep. Whenever they came knocking on the door, Aunt Grace will say, "Kenn go and tell them that I have gone to the market". Then I will innocently go, "Aunty Grace says I should come and tell you that she has gone to the market" "you mean she sent you out to tell us that she's not around?" "No", "she said she has gone to the market." At this point, they will burst out laughing while I will be left wondering what I have done that has created such uncontrollable laughter.

Many children are victims of the same experience. So many parents and carers have turned their home to a training ground for liars and deceivers only to turn around and blame their children for diligently taking after their foot step. It is wrong. **Don't wish your child to be godly, show him how to be godly.**

Does your child see you as a father or a mere male personality around the house? This is a question every "father" must answer. **You are not yet a father because you have a child, what defines fatherhood is the responsibility of nurturing, correcting, impacting and inculcating the godly and moral values that makes a child a plus to his or her community.**

Lamenting on the declining state of male role models in the family, the first black president of the United State, Barack Obama, in his speech on the annual father's day in America on 15th June, 2008 as observed by Babatunde Adedibu, *Storytelling An Effective Communication Appeal In Preaching,* has this to say, "too many fathers are also missing—missing from too many lives and too many homes. They have abandoned their responsibilities, acting like boys instead of men and the foundation of their family has suffered because of it" Obama continued by pointing out that **"what makes you a man is not the ability to have a child—it's the courage to raise one".**

Speaking with the same passion, a Higher Education Minister, David Lammy as quoted by Vanessa Maynard in Voice newspaper of 26th March, 2010 was of the opinion that "children do better when their fathers are involved in their lives". Drawing on his personal experience and feelings of betrayal when his own father left him at the age of twelve, Lammy opined that children without active fathers are more likely to face problems.

The basic truth here is the understanding that the greatest investment any parent can make is to invest in the positive upbringing of their children, shaping them to be positive influence to their peers, depositing in them the values and morals that will make them the pride of their society and the beloved of their creator. Until this is achieved, your future peace is not guaranteed.

PART FOUR

BUILDING YOUR HOME WITH THE RIGHT BUILDING BLOCKS

"My belief is that a successful marriage is built one moment at a time. From what I've learned, a marriage is like a stone wall: it's a mix of big things and little things, all assembled together to form something strong. Sure, there are a lot of big rocks in that wall (the big moments in your marriage, like your wedding day or some other big, key moment), but those rocks don't fit together without a lot of little rocks to fill in the gaps and make them strong."
TRENT HAMM

CHAPTER 10

Punishment or Discipline?

God does not punish His children, he disciplines them.
Punishment is for those who despise discipline.

You are not permitted to hate your child even though you may not necessarily like his or her behaviour. The Bible recommends discipline for children and not punishment. Punishment is cruel, selfish and often amounts to abuse. On the contrary, discipline is a proof of love and care for one's children. When discipline is done without love and care or with selfish purpose, it becomes punishment and that is abuse. Discipline is a part and parcel of the growth and development of the child. The Bible has it in Heb.12:11:

> "Now no chastening (discipline) for the present
> seemeth to be joyous, but grievous: nevertheless
> afterward it yielded the peaceable fruit of righteousness
> unto them which are exercised thereby.

Sometimes ago in my family, my wife and I observed that one of our sons had developed an uncontrollable appetite for meat. It became more embarrassing when he exhibits it outside our home or in the midst of visitors. One of the days, my wife visited a family friend and my children went with her, the same attitude was exhibited. She then thought of the suitable discipline that could discourage him from the habit and eventually decided he wasn't going to have meat for days. I supported her and that was the secret that brought the change. There are different ways children can be disciplined with effective output. These include temporally denying them of some privileges and benefits, depending on the age of the child.

Physical discipline should be the last resort, yet it must be done with maximum caution with the intention to correct. Reward for good behaviour and attitude is considered more effective in child training than outright punishment. The motivating factor for disciplining a child should be for the purpose of effecting positive change in the child and not for parental selfish interest.

> *". . . for what child is he whom the father chasteneth not? But if you be without chastisement, wherefore all are partakers, then are ye bastards, and not sons. Furthermore, we have had fathers of our flesh which corrected us, and we gave them reverence. Shall we not much rather be in subjection unto the father of spirits, and live?* **For they verily for a few days chastened us after their own pleasure . . .**"
> Heb. 12:7-10

The greatest mistake parents make is to think that they will produce children who will never make mistakes. Such parents have zero tolerance for their children's mistakes. When you allow love for perfection determines your love for your children, you are heading towards abuse. A loving father or mother will expect and make room for their children's mistake.

It is child abuse to deny your child love, joy, happiness, care and the needed attention they deserve in the name of punishment. On the other hand, refusal to discipline your child or children when they choose a wrong path of life can also amount to child abuse. For me, **the proper definition of child abuse is a refusal to train up a child in the way of God.** Many children grow up in highly "toxic household" where abuse and violence has become a way of life.

SIX MAJOR ABUSE CHILDREN GO THROUGH

Researchers have been able to discover five major ways through which children are abused, but have failed either deliberately or ignorantly to point out the sixth one which is the most important: **spiritual abuse.** For the purpose of deeper understanding, we shall briefly study these abuses.

Physical Abuse

Physical abuse occurs when children are non-accidentally injured by adults thereby causing physical harm or ill health. So many children go through all manners of reckless hitting, smacking, shaking, caning, throwing, kicking, burning, poisoning, scalding, drowning and suffocating in the hands of the adults who ought to protect them. In the process, some children are left with permanent bruises, scars and in some cases, death. I read the news in the internet of a father who beat his seven years child to death in Nigeria for what he termed "lost of temper".

In as much as the Bible recommends discipline, this should be used as a tool for correction and not to punish or inflict injuries. Such attitude will rather make your children grow with hatred and become rebellious to you and may lose faith in God as well. Children who are victims of domestic violence grow up to be violent themselves. I read another story where a mother was teaching her daughter how to read and write. At a point, the starving daughter could not take in any further teaching and the mother "lost her temper". She came back to her senses after realizing that she has beaten her daughter to death. Restraint must be exercised in child discipline. Sometimes, children may push parents too far in their attitude; nevertheless, they are still children while we are adults.

Emotional Abuse

Emotional abuse occurs when children are denied affection and love. The reason why God allowed your children to come into the world through you is because He knows that you can care for them. Don't let God down. Children that are nurtured under a loving environment often grow up to be loving adults and blessings to the society. No one can give what he or she does not have; this is why the society moves in a vicious circle: unloved children growing up to give birth to children who are yet deprived of affection.

When you constantly shout at your children, threatening, teasing and taunting them, it is a sign of abuse. Some parents are good at creating fear in their children, exposing them to danger thereby making them to grow with a sense of insecurity, fear and distrust. Domestic violence, bullying and favouring a child above others creates emotional abuse.

The problem the brothers of Joseph had in Gen.37 was not just a problem of jealousy; they were victims of emotional abuse. They witnessed Jacob their father showering his unreserved love to Rachael while their own mother Leah was despised and had to beg before she can spend a night with her husband. As if that was not enough, when Joseph was born, Jacob never pretended or for one day concealed his superior love for him. Do you know that he even sewed a coat of many colours for him? Unknown to Jacob, he was tormenting his other children emotionally; he ended up sowing a seed of hatred and jealousy in their hearts towards Joseph. **Don't be careless in your affection for your children by letting them feel that you are partial in your love towards them.**

Neglect

Children can be abused through neglect and negligence. Neglect occurs when parents refuse to provide basic needs to their children. You don't have to be very wealthy to have the needs of your children met. The greatest need of a child is the need for attention. I learnt a lesson when my son Praise was very young. I had to be a nursing father because his mum travelled out the country for a long period. In the process, he got so used to me that he never spared me a moment of independence. After a while, I started leaving him in the care of a child minder to enable me go to the church to pray and to prepare for the church programmes; I was then the head pastor of a church denomination.

One of the days, I was set to go and Praise ran after me "Daddy, where are you going?" He asked with all seriousness and eagerness to get an answer. "To the church, Yoyo" was my response as I approached the door. "What are you going to do in the church?" Praise asked now displaying some concern. I paused to think of a more suitable answer to give to a three years old child, I eventually answered, "I want to go and talk with God". I was now smiling, thinking that the mention of God will create the right feeling in his heart, but no, Praise looked at my face, fixing his eyes to catch my attention and then bent his neck "why not bring God home". At that point, it became obvious to me that my son needs nothing but my attention and my time; it appears to him that going to church takes my attention away from him, so he suggested then that I bring God home. Praise won because God was in the house with us that day as He has always been. Your child needs your attention.

So many children are denied parental attention, good clothing {not necessarily expensive}, good food, warmth, guidance and supervision. This is neglect, and it is child abuse. Failure to protect and defend your children from danger is an indication of abuse. Also, pulling your children out of school to hawk on the street and do certain jobs and career is child abuse. Such activities give them a false sense of maturity which is destructive and does not promote integrity. The soul of your children is precious in the sight of God and you shall give account of what you did with them.

Sexual Abuse

Today, the media is flooded by shocking news of paedophiles and child sex offenders, but it is even more shameful and shocking to discover that children are sometimes sexually abused by their own parents. This is an abominable act before God. A situation where children are shamelessly exposed to sexual activities either through the movies they watch with minimal supervision or by engaging them in unpleasant sexual experiences defines sexual abuse.

Parents and adults in general should exercise restraint in the kind of words and acts they exhibit in the presence of children. This is because children are often very fast in picking and practising the things they observe adults do. Children who grow up as victims of child abuse often give back to the society what the society deposited in them. They grow up with a psychological determination to be victors and not victims any longer by abusing others sexually. This is one of the fundamental reasons for increase in rape activities.

Spiritual Abuse

> *"And the Lord said to Samuel, Behold, I will do a thing in Israel, at which both the ears of every one that heareth it shall tingle. In that day, I will perform against Eli all things which*

> *I have spoken concerning his house: when I begin, I will also make an end. For I have told him that I will judge his house for ever for the iniquity which he knoweth;* **because his sons made themselves vile, and he restrained them not".**
> 1 Sam.3:11-13

More dangerous than every other abuse is spiritual abuse. To abuse a child spiritually is to deny that child spiritual nurturing that will make a positive effect in his or her relationship with God. There are three ways parents find themselves trading the path of spiritual abuse: being silent even when your child has chosen to live an ungodly lifestyle, being nonchalant about the choices made by your child most especially in relation to morals, and displaying weak attitude in correcting your child in the name of encouraging self esteem and love.

Spiritual abuse can be active or passive. There are active child abusers and passive child abusers. Learning from Eli's case, he was not actively involved in the spiritual abuse of his children, but he was a passive abuser thus God said, "he restrained them (his children) not". It is unfortunate that parents, who abuse children spiritually, will not be spared from giving an account before their Maker. Man is not only a physical or emotional being, but a spiritual being. As a result a deeper relationship with God is what will determine the child's well being.

In Gen.18:17-19, God boasted about Abraham simply because he will not abuse his children:

> *"And the Lord said, shall I hide from Abraham that thing which I do; seeing that Abraham shall surely become a great and mighty nation, and all the nations of the earth shall be blessed in him?* ***for I know him that he will command his children and his house hold after him, and they shall keep the way of the Lord, to do justice and judgement; that the Lord may bring upon Abraham that which he hath spoken of him."***

The reason for the increase in juvenile offences and vices in the society today is as a result of blackout in spiritual training from the home. *"The fear of the Lord is the beginning of wisdom".* Children should be taught to depend on God for solution to the challenges of life; they should be made to understand that every other thing may fail, but when they put their trust in the lord, victory is assured.

But how can parents give what they don't have, how can they encourage their children to know God when their (parents) hearts are spiritually bankrupt? It is expected that every parent wakes up spiritually at least for the sake of your children. For me, **the greatest gift I owe my children is the gift of salvation.**

PART FIVE

CEILING YOUR MARRIAGE WITH LOVE

A woman is like a door, she has got what it takes to take you to paradise or right to the pit of hell. Flee from adultery.

CHAPTER 11

Sex and Romance in Marriage

Where's All the Romance Gone?

"How fair is thy love, my sister, my spouse! How much better is thy love than wine! and the smell of thy ointment than all spices! Thy lips o my spouse, drop as the honeycomb: honey and milk are under thy tongue; and the smell of thy garments is like the smell of Lebanon. A garden inclosed is my sister, my spouse: a spring shut up, a fountain sealed."
Songs of Sol. 4:10-12

Sex and romance is an expression of the highest form of intimacy for married couples. It is a very important aspect of marriage, don't live it for the unmarried. Many couples have become so "spiritually minded" that they have abandon romance for the world. To be a romantic husband or wife does not make you less spiritual; on the contrary, it is a proof of your maturity and understanding of your responsibility to your spouse. There is nothing sinful about sex and romance for couples, rather it is a sin to shy away from it; in fact it is your test of maturity. Sex and romance become unacceptable only when it is wrongly practiced. **Sex in marriage is not a chore but a thing of pleasure.**

You might have problems in your marriage if you are not a romantic husband or wife. The excuse some men give mostly in Africa for shying away from this God licensed practice for couple is that they don't want to be labelled as "woman wrapper"; if being a romantic husband is interpreted as being "a woman wrapper", I choose to be more romantic. The desire for sex and romance is God's gift to couple. It is expected that a man should learn to cuddle and kiss his wife as much as he can and not only when he desires sex.

THE IMPORTANCE OF SEX AND ROMANCE IN MARRIAGE

Sex and romance is part of God's design for marriage: God designed sex for those within the confine of marital union as a positive way of driving the engine of marital intimacy forward and offering an avenue for reproduction and procreation.

> *"How fair is thy love, my sister, my spouse! How much better is thy love than wine! and the smell of thy ointment than all spices! Thy lips o my spouse, drop as the honeycomb: honey and milk are under thy tongue; and the smell of thy garments is like the smell of Lebanon. A garden inclosed is my sister, my spouse: a spring shut up, a fountain sealed."*
> Songs of Sol. 4:10-12

> *"Marriage is honourable in all, and the bed undefiled: but whoremongers and adulterers God will judge.*
> *"Heb.13:4*

It may appear shocking to realize that God is actually interested in man's sexual activities. From the above verses, it is obvious that the scripture encourages sexual pleasure and enjoyment between two married couples—a man and woman, yet He frowns at promiscuity. He created our parts and aesthetically designed the body organs to respond to sexual stimuli.

IGNITING THE FIRE OF ROMANCE

> "The most often-reported reason for a dying marriage was not because couples fought too often or because there'd been an affair, but because they grew apart and there was deadness between them."
> **Linda and Robert Miles.**

Romance is the fuel that keeps marital love burning, though it is not a complete proof of love, yet it provokes an emotional bond between a man and a woman, it is the oil that lubricates your union and keep the wheels of marriage rolling. **When romance is dead in your marriage, love suffers.** Romance dies when couples stop doing those things that gives them joy during courtship: the places they love visiting together, the way they played and prayed together, the wonderful names they called each other, the dressing, make ups and perfumes that gave them approval during courtship.

> *"Let thy fountain be blessed: and rejoice with the wife of thy youth. Let her be as the loving hind and pleasant roe; let her breasts satisfy you at all times; and be thou ravished always with her love. And why wilt thou, my son, be ravished with a strange woman, and embrace the bosom of a stranger?"*
> *Prov. 5:18-20 says:*

One of the wonderful ways of igniting the romantic passion in your marriage is by reassuring your spouse that you love and accept him or her for who they are and how they look; it creates a sense of appreciation and approval. This is cemented through loving touch, care and caress. The more body contacts you enjoy in your marriage, the more you cherish each other and your marriage is secured and warm. Body contact must not necessarily end up with sex; it reassures your spouse of that sense of care, possession and appreciation for each other. Touching is a form of communication. Read this:

> **"When physical problems are not the root cause of a diminished sex life, many remedies exist to rekindle the flame of passion. Much of the fix is grounded in communication and re-prioritizing one's life to make time for love and sex"**
> ***Jan Sinatra,***

Couples must be genuine and honest about sex and romance with each other. Avoid using sex as a bargaining tool or as a weapon. Don't manipulate your spouse through sexual acceptance or refusal.

According to Gearon, from 2001 and 2004 statistics, it was revealed that couples are often too tired to have sex. "The 2010 Sleep in America Poll reports that one in four Americans say they are too sleepy and their sexual relationship is affected. Still others may just need to build time into their schedules to be together and let nature takes its course. Simply setting aside date nights can jump-start one's love life"

THE ROMANTIC HUSBAND

Are you a romantic husband? I think the most qualified person to answer this question is your wife. A friend once told me a story about visiting a couple in his church. He got into family discussion with the man and the topic centred on love. They shared their experiences about how lovely their marriages have been. Unknown to the host, his wife was in their room listening to all their conversation. She suddenly came out of the room and said to her husband, "Darling, please when people talk about love, can you just be quiet". My friend could not hold his laughter as the embarrassed husband covered his face in shame. After that visit and counselling offered by my friend, romance, peace and joy were restored to that home. Do you forget your wife's birthday? Then you're not a romantic husband.

Romance Starts from the Kitchen

Romance in marriage is not all about hugging and kissing, but doing kind deeds and saying kind words to each other. Join your wife in doing some domestic chores and volunteer to prepare the family meal sometimes; you can also do the dishes or laundry as a way of encouraging her. Some traditions and cultures have made it almost a taboo for a man to enter the kitchen or support his wife with domestic chores. I may have to disappoint you by telling you that times has changed; **romance starts from the kitchen and ends in the bed room.**

From research, most women are of the opinion that their husbands are romantic when

- they are sensitive to their wife's feelings
- they are good listeners during conversation
- they are caring and loving

- they are sharing and encouraging
- they tolerate their wife's imperfections
- they enjoy and are attracted to their wife's body
- they are playful and tender intelligent and supportive
- they are funny and protective
- They show understanding.

THE ROMANTIC WIFE

A romantic wife is the one that treats her husband as the king which he is. Such a wife knows that her husband comes first before any other person including her children. The moment a woman starts competing with her husband and usurps his authority in the home, she loses her romantic nature. A bossy and nagging attitude from women is a major destroyer of romance in the home.

Some years ago when I was in the university, we used to have a sister who was the Secretary General of our Campus Christian Fellowship. Margaret was so pretty, caring, matured, but she has this bossy, authoritarian and almost a dictatorship kind of character which also reflected in her leadership. One of the days, few of the "brothers" were in the male hostel chatting. Of course it was not strange that our subject of discussion was marriage. We had this funny brother who insisted that he was looking for a wife from our fellowship. Jokingly, we started sampling and mentioning some names for his approval. Suddenly, somebody suggested Margaret and the countenance of the brother changed. With a loud hiss he uttered "I said I am looking for a wife and not a husband". Every one could not hold their laughter but a message was communicated.

A romantic wife will never try to take the place of the man in the home; she is supportive and willing to satisfy his needs most especially his sexual need. By nature, God designed women to be romantic. Women are more romantic than men; this often manifests in their attitude and the things that appeal to them. While men are carried away by pressure and busy schedules of life, women could be busy as well but less likely to forget keeping with her dates, holidays, honeymoon, birthdays and the rest of them. Some days ago, I called my brother on the phone to wish him happy birthday. It was just a day after his birthday but to my shock, he totally forgot it was his birthday. He was almost embarrassed when I said happy birthday to him. Few women, if not none will forget such days.

A romantic wife is also known by her dressing. You don't necessarily have to be sophisticated in your dressing, yet you should not be a slob around your husband? Try dressing nice for him in such a way that his eyes will never wander away. From research, some of the qualities that make a romantic wife include:

- Mature in attitude
- Honest and truthful
- Caring and kind
- Neat and well dressed
- Good listeners
- Intelligent and wise
- Beautiful and have good body
- Emotional and warm
- Affectionate and friendly
- Humorous and outgoing
- Desirous and needful of their husband
- Understanding and submissive.

The list of wife's and husband's expectations from their spouses is never absolute. You are free to outline your own points but it is very important for me to warn that you should not use these lists to judge or condemn your spouse. It is for the purpose of self development.

DEROMANTICISATION

I think the greatest killer of marriage in developed world is job factor. Many men and women are married to their job, spending more time, devotion and commitment to their job more than to their union and family. The more long hours we work, the more tired we become. The result is less romance, less intimacy, less understanding and more alienation leading to separation and marriage breakdown. Couples must find a way of making it up to each other; think about setting aside days or weeks to be with each other. If you have the means, arrange and plan for family holidays and make it romantic.

There are some nasty and careless habits that destroy romance in marriage, and couples should be careful about this. It is insensitivity not to border about those habits that makes your spouse uncomfortable. For Most spouses, nasty habits show a lack of respect and they can lead to lack of romance in a marriage. It is often believed that men are more prone to careless attitudes and habits that sometimes violet behavioural norm.

Sometime ago in Africa, I heard a story of a marriage that broke down because of the size of the ball of pounded yam that the man moulds in his palm during dinner and how he swallows it. This may appear funny, but it is quite serious. I guess the marriage broke down when intolerance from the wife met with insensitivity from the husband.

But some women are also in this same mess of nasty habits. Some nasty habits may be smoking, drunkenness, dirtiness nagging, yelling and many others. Minor issues like the careless fondling of tooth paste when brushing one's teeth, wet towels on bathroom floors and other nasty habits may create mild discomfort, but repeated occurrence may lead to unfavourable reaction.

WHEN SEX BECOMES A TABOO

". . . but whoremongers and adulterers God will judge."
Heb. 13:4

It is important to note that when one indulges in sexual promiscuity, some part of you is lost to a stranger. It is a terrible sin to God, to mankind and to your body as well. This is because in every intercourse, there is a sharing of feelings, emotions, passion, and above all, a part of you is transferred. God in His infinite wisdom structured the chemistry of the human body to derive pleasure from sex and romance. When you engage in premarital or extra marital sex, it becomes an abuse of divine privilege and an abomination to God. For a decent society, this is a taboo.

Finally, building an unshakable home is a highest level of sacrifice; the responsibility to turn your marriage "for better" or "for worse" is yours. If you don't do something, nothing gets done.

BIBLIOGRAPHY

Aranza Jacob "Lord, Why Is My Child a Rebel?"

Adedibu, Babatunde, 2009, *Storytelling an Effective Communication Appeal in Preaching,* the Choir Press

Barnett R. Brickner in QuoteGarden.com, quoted in Sheri and Bob Stritof, 2010 *"Your guide to Marriage"* About.com

Ikeda, Daisaku *"Love and Marriage-Words of Wisdom"* Soka Gakkai
David Lammy quoted by Vanessa Maynard, Voice newspaper of 26th March, 2010

Doug Larson *"Garden.com."*

Hagee, John and Diana, 2005, *What Every Man Wants in a Woman, What Every Woman Wants in a Man,* 10 Qualities of Nurturing Intimacy, United State of America, Marriage—Religious Aspect.

Jan Sinatra, Heart Sense for Women. Quoted in Christopher J. Gearon.: "Sex in Marriage: Better Sex in Marriage." Health Discovery.com

Leno, Mavis, in Jeanne Wolf., 1999, *Reconcilable differences,* Redbook.

Leno, Mavis: quoted in Sue Smalley, 2009. *"Happily ever laughter."* LATimes.com

Macionis, John, J, 1991, *Sociology,* Third Edition, Prentice Hall, Inc.

Meredith, Roderick, C, 2006, *God's Plan for Happy Marriage,* United State of America, Living Church of God.

Miles, Linda and Robert 2000: *The New Marriage: Transcending the Happily-Ever-After Myth*

Paul Newman Your guide to Marriage"

Rose Campbell "How to Really Love Your Teenager"

Roesch 1984:75

Roderick C Meredith, *God's Plan for a Happy Marriage* Pg.22 "

Stewart, Mary. 1972. *"Book has no easy answers."* The Argus.

Sheri, Bob Stritof, 2010: *"Your guide to Marriage"*. About.com

Susanna, Stefanachi Macomb. 2010 *"Renewing Wedding Vows—Examples and Sample Vows for a Wedding Vow Renewal Ceremony—The Why, Where, When & How of Renewing Wedding Vows"* About.com

Trent Hamm *"Some thoughts on building a successful marriage"*

Tola Onigbanjo: "Seven Biggest Mistakes Parents Make".

Warren, Rick, 2002: *The purpose driven life,* Grand Rapids, Michigan

Voice newspaper, 26 March, 2010

ABOUT THE BOOK

This is a book for all tastes. The skilful craft of a novel contains advice, humour and romance in a neat religious package that is not only entertaining and romantic but challenges the reader's mind and imagination of the total concept of marriage.

Dr. Frank Gyan-Amponsah
Researcher/Senior Lecturer (Economics & Management)
London
UK

I recommend this to every married couple and those contemplating to build a viable home through Christian type of marriage or any other type of marriage . . . It is highly recommended for every library and all who cherish the marriage institution.

Ven. Obioma Onwuzurumba
Chaplain, Aso Villa Chapel. Abuja, Nigeria.

Building an unshakable home is a highest level of sacrifice; the responsibility to turn your marriage "for better" or "for worse" is yours. In ***My Beautiful Garden***, Kenn Mark elaborates on an important field which forms the basic foundation for human existence—marriage and family life. Your choice of a life partner will go a long way in determining and shaping your destiny on earth. The chapters are segmented to answer the questions of both the married and unmarried readers: Children, preachers, marriage counsellors and every one who truly desires guidance for building a joyful home.

ABOUT THE AUTHOR

Kenn Mark is a motivational writer. He emphasizes on secret of success. He is committed to healing relationships and building solid marriage and family life as well as raising leaders through his message of Dominion. Kenn Mark pastors with the Redeemed Christian Church of God in United Kingdom

RE: MY BEAUTIFUL GARDEN

REVIEW

I am honoured that you allowed me to pre-read your manuscript, MY BEAUTIFUL GARDEN. I was spellbound! The story is woven of the elements I honour most in my life. The book was more than we could have imagined. Both Naomi and I could not put it down. In fact we were scrambling over whose turn it was to read it. She beat me to it and finished first.

The book really grabbed me and I read until it was finished, couldn't put it down. I love it. The months of research that you put into writing it certainly paid off, it was great! I have always been fascinated with books on marriage and this has gone a long way to increase my understanding and knowledge about marriage. Your narrations of BUILDING YOUR HOME ON THE RIGHT FOUNDATION were especially well written and captured my full attention. In addition, it was both interesting and informative to become acquitted with the richness of WHAT`S SPECIAL ABOUT HOME and PILLARS OF MARRIAGE.

This is a book for all tastes. This skilful craft of a novel contains advice, humour and romance in a neat religious package that is not only entertaining and romantic but challenges the reader's mind and imagination of the total concept of marriage.

MY BEAUTIFUL GARDEN is a delight to read. One can only hope that from a writer of this talent, there will be many more books to come. The book is a masterful blend of advice, lessons and ways to enjoy one's marriage, with liberal dashes of humour and generous pinches of wit bound together by a stirring romance that not only transcends time but forever binds present to past. Using the backdrop of both scripture and modern day contemporary issues of marriage, each page grabs you and prepares you for the next.

Brimming with rich scripturally accurate details, spontaneous sequence of five different vivid parts makes this a book you will not be able to put down!

Bravo Pastor Mark! I'm looking forward to your next book.

Dr. Frank Gyan-Amponsah
Researcher/Senior Lecturer (Economics & Management)
London
UK